W9-AZP-916

Kathe — Always Been in Norway

Espen Søbye: *Kathe - Always Been in Norway*
Original Title: *Kathe – Alltid vært i Norge* (Norway, 2003)
Translated by Kerri Pierce
English edition 2019

Copyright © 2019 by Krakiel Publishing

All rights reserved. Published by Krakiel Publishing, Oslo, Norway
www.krakielforlag.no
ISBN 978-82-997381-2-5

FSC
Printed on Holmen Book Cream 1.8 FSC
Cover design: Concorde Design
Cover Photo: Private
Printed in Latvia.

N
NORLA
This translation has been published with the financial support of NORLA

All Rights reserved. No part of this publication may be reproduced or
transmitted in any form or by any means, electronic or mechanical, including
photocopying, recording, or by any information storage and retrieval system,
without written permission from the publisher.

ESPEN SØBYE

Kathe – Always Been in Norway

Translated by Kerri Pierce

With an introduction by Sarah Wildman

KRAKIEL

CONTENT

We are not eyewitnesses.

Foreword by SARAH WILDMAN

We did not experience the war. We did not see atrocities. We did not try to escape, nor did we help others escape.

We are of the generations born after. We are those for whom the stories of the Nazi era have always been exactly that: stories. But we do have one thing that many of our children will not: we have spoken to those who saw.

***

In the spring of 2015, I was invited by a synagogue in New York City to participate in their Yom HaShoah – Holocaust Memorial Day – service. At the beginning of the evening, name after name was intoned with gravity and solemnity; each a prayer, of sorts. Throughout the recitation, individuals rose, silently, and put matches to wicks. Soon the stage was filled with flickering candles; the effect was that of a burning, mournful sea.

Throughout the ceremony, I found myself wondering who the people on the list were. Some in the sanctuary that evening were children, grandchildren, or spouses of survivors; names on the list with connection to that group were read first. But mostly the names were presented without even the small definition of familial relationship, or biographical detail. Was this name that of a mother? A grandmother? An adult? A child?

There is an accidental cruelty in the reduction of a life to a memorial list; it is, however unintentionally, a form of erasure. For what is a name, alone, devoid of context, devoid of property, of distinction, bereft of those who loved that name? And yet what can one do?

So often, understandably, in our history texts we focus on the Nazi efforts to exterminate the six million Jews. But the Nazis weren't bent on simple bodily destruction. Their intent was erasure, the destruction of individual identities. The lists of victims' names, inadvertently, reinforce that obliteration. The weight of the lines of text, all those lost, all those names, becomes a blur, offering precious little insight into lives lived.

In the early post-war years, the vastness of the genocide precluded investigations into individual stories outside of a few notable cases. This made sense. The world needed the recitation of events, a setting down for future generations of the full arc of the history. The horror was so improbable in its size that the scope of the terror needed to be hammered upon, again and again.

But in the subsequent waves of historiography, the lives of regular people, the destruction of their persons and their property, have come to be understood as nearly equally important as the number of people murdered and the number of murderous camps. Indeed, individual stories become, as each year passes, an essential access point to understanding the history. There is a yearning among historians and educators for contemporary letters, diaries, personal testimony.

It was the importance of the very specific details of a single life that Espen Søbye so well understood when he came across the name Kathe Lasnik.

But at first all he had was a name, and an age. He had no context; no letters, no diaries – no means of knowing her. In telling her story he has accomplished both a means of rescue, and a modern form of witnessing. Indeed, in this book, Søbye has given a model for those of us concerned with this history, and the loss of eyewitnesses. He has provided a path for those who search for ways to ensure this history will not be forgotten. He has allowed the documents, and the city streets of Oslo, to speak. In so doing he has also illuminated a geographic corner of this dark history that most of us in the English-speaking world have rarely, if ever, considered.

**

On October 13, 1927, a girl was born in Oslo. Her parents, Elias and Dora Lasnik, immigrants from Vilna who had lived in Norway for nineteen years, named her Kathe Rita. She was raised cocooned in a family that had steadily, impressively, improved its lot since the early 1900s. Her parents claimed Norwegian citizenship not long after her birth.

Kathe missed their hardscrabble years, years with no indoor toilet and rudimentary kitchens while her father toiled as a tinsmith and her mother worked, first in a tobacco factory, and then as a fruit seller. By the time of her childhood, Kathe's far older siblings were contributing to the household, her parents had been able to take on household help from time to time, and life had settled into a rhythm of normalcy.

Kathe, too, would likely have continued to live a quiet Norwegian existence had she not had the misfortune of having her childhood intersect with the Nazi occupation of her home country.

The world would surely know nothing of Kathe, were it not for Espen Søbye. And even Søbye came across Kathe's name quite by accident. Though he had written many books, and though he was already quite well known in Norway for his literature, he had yet to touch on the Jewish history of the Second World War. In fact, it was not because of his writing, but because of his work at Statistics Norway that he was asked by William Seltzer of Fordham University to look into the role of statistics in the deportation of the Jews of Norway.

Unsurprisingly, given the Nazi predilection for precise record keeping, it turned out that statistics, sober, dry, played a profound role in the destruction of Norway's small Jewish community. Take the letter J: Søbye discovered the Norwegian police had placed an order for 700 rubber stamps of the letter J – with a precise shape and size – a collection meant to be sent to police stations across Norway. A small statistic: 700 rubber stamps. An order filled in response to the occupation. This was not, however, an order for office supplies; instead it was the first step in ethnic cleansing. Each would be used to mark the papers of the Jews, to separate them.

In his initial foray into these statistics, Søbye also came across some 1,419 questionnaires filled out by Norwegian Jews in 1942. The documents were still held in the archives of the Ministry of the Police. The forms, which ultimately came to serve the nefarious purpose of identification for collection and deportation, all asked the Jews: "When did you come to Norway?" The assumption was, of course, that Jews were not indigenous to Norway at all.

There were many, many forms Søbye might have stopped to read, but it was that of 15-year-old Kathe that caught his eye. On her form she answered the question "When did you come to Norway?" with a simple phrase: "I've always been in Norway." It is one of the few sentences we have from her pen.

Such few words: *I've always been in Norway*. And yet it speaks – with a young voice – to so much: the petty bureaucracy of persecution, her own national identity – upended by racial and racist policies – and the undeniable destruction of a sense of self and place.

This fragment of a sentence is also a pointed finger. Søbye explains that the questionnaire that Kathe filled out – in triplicate – along with all her fellow *landsmen* was created not by the Gestapo, but by the Statistics Office of her own home country.

Some 1100 Jews were spirited from Norway into safety in Sweden. Most left with the help of, and great personal risk to, the Norwegian underground resistance, a robust and vibrant underground that actively fought the Quisling government – named for the eager collaborator Vidkun Quisling, whose very name, post-war, would come to symbolize betrayal of country.

Søbye's book focuses not upon that heroism but, instead, he swings our attention to view the other half of Norway's war story: how the separation of many of Norway's Jews from Norwegian society, and then their deportation, was aided immeasurably by networks of local police and official agencies who not only failed the Jews, but actually facilitated their undoing by carrying out Gestapo orders of ethnic cleansing with heartless efficiency.

Nearly 800 Norwegian Jews were excised from their cities, their society, their country. They were deported to death camps, and murdered.

***

To some degree it was not strange that the Jews of Norway were so quickly and easily separated from society, that they were so easily disentangled from the world around them.

Norway's history with Jews was very short – Article 2 of the 1814 Constitution forbade Jews from entering the country at all. It was only in 1851 that that Jews were welcome in Norway, and even then, few arrived. It was some decades after that that Jews chose to settle in Norway, a lag which meant Jews were never fully integrated in Norwegian society.

In the 1920s and 1930s, debates raged in Norway about kashrut, the Jewish dietary restrictions, and, specifically, rules for slaughtering animals. (It was deemed cruel to animals; the debates were decidedly anti-Semitic in tone). Other moments of Jew-baiting would crop up from time to time. Starting in 1935, Quisling, then a minor party leader, and his followers spoke of the "Jewish problem" and his racist ranting regarding Jews in society sounded akin to the rhetoric of Nazi Germany.[1]

Jews, therefore, weren't clearly as fully integrated in Norway as they were elsewhere in Western Europe. Most Norwegians simply did not know Jews. So the vast majority of Norwegians did not know them as neighbors, or colleagues, or part of the texture of Norwegian society.

Germany occupied Norway in April 1940. Within two years, as elsewhere in occupied Europe, Jews began to be singled out and persecuted. Stores were smeared with anti-Semitic slogans; Jewish musicians were banned from performances. By 1942 Jews were stripped of professional titles. Radios were taken away. News of the outside world itself became contraband – listening to the BBC was illegal,

---

[1]   Samuel Abrahamsen. "Norway's Response to the Holocaust: A Historical Perspective." Copyright 1991 p. 48

and detailing to neighbors what you had heard on a foreign broadcast a punishable offense.[2]

In January 1942, police stations across Norway put their J stamps to use: each Jew was required to have a "J" embossed upon his papers, marking each as an outsider. In February of that year Jews were asked to fill out those terrible questionnaires. Frantically, many Jews sought passage to Sweden, taking great risks to travel by foot and by boat, using the cover of night.

"We are a race of martyrs," wrote Ruth Maier, a Viennese diarist who had lived in Norway since her escape from Vienna two years before.[3] In October 1942, the Quisling government declared that Jewish property was no longer Jewish property, but state property, and thus could be seized.[4]

Police departments across the country received telegrams with precise instructions for carrying out the first mass arrests of Jewish men on October 25;[5] the following morning, early, police officers in task forces fanned out to pick up boys and their fathers across the country.[6] This first group of Jewish inmates was held for a month in atrocious conditions, in camps on Norwegian soil.

On November 25, K. A. Marthinsen, head of the Norwegian State Police, alerted police across the country that Jewish women and children would be rounded up the following day. The women would then join their men and be sent away from Norway. "I received orders from the German security police," Marthinsen later wrote, as Samuel Abrahamsen reprinted in his masterful text *Norway's Response to the Holocaust,* "that all Jews with a 'J' stamped on their identification cards, as well as their families, should be evacuated from Norway."[7]

---

2   Hans Frederick Dahl. "Quisling: A Study in Treachery." Cambridge. 2008. p. 283

3   Ruth Maier's Diary. Edited by Jan Erik Vold. Copyright 2010. p. 406

4   https://www.regjeringen.no/en/dokumenter/white_paper_no_82_1997-98/id201553/

5   Abrahamsen, p. 104

6   Abrahamsen, pp. 110-111

7   Abrahamsen, p. 118

Søbye discovered that every man from the state police force was called in; forty more were added from the Oslo criminal police, and 20 from the German SS itself.

The ship waiting for the trapped Jews in the harbor was the S.S. Donau, which was set to sail from Oslo to Stettin on the Baltic coast. Norway would soon have the dubious distinction – alongside Greece – of being one of only two European countries to deport its Jews by boat.

By all reports, the scenes at the port were brutal and heart-wrenching.

The passage of the S.S. Donau took longer than anticipated. There were storms. Food rations brought on board were not handed out to the prisoners. And as Espen Søbye points out, the Norwegian authorities likely already knew that the destination was not work or resettlement, but terrible danger, and even death. Already in August of 1942 the Swedish consul in the Baltic seaport town of Stettin had reported on the use of gas, and on mass slaughter.

Among the bewildered and terrified Jews gathered on the S.S. Donau were Kathe, her mother, her father and one sister. Two sisters had escaped to freedom. A family divided, like so many others. When Søbye sat to visit with the surviving sisters, it was hard to ask the questions he had come to investigate. How do you ask about the lost? How do you probe such a wound?

***

"I thought it was terrible that Kathe Lasnik was only remembered because she had been a victim," Søbye muses at the beginning of his search. "Was there perhaps someone out there who could remember her for something more?" But at first all he could find were references to Kathe on lists of the dead, and on memorials. He scoured the documents of Norway for every mention of her, or her family. He walked to the buildings she lived in, the schools she attended; he saw how the architecture of Oslo held her story, waiting to be told.

The story of Kathe Lasnik, recounted in these pages, is a heroic effort to rescue a single person from the depths of obscurity, to restore the dignity of individuality stolen from a girl who had not yet made her mark on the world. Her family was not wealthy, so they did not own great art or major property. Their goods were looted, but for petty cash; nothing remains of their property. Her writings were not collected in a diary.

With frustratingly few clues in hand, Søbye was determined to find all that he could. He wanted the details of daily life; he wanted eyewitness accounts of her after-school activities. He tracked down Kathe's two surviving relatives; he found old schoolmates, neighbors, maids. Then, using the administrative details of the destruction of her people – the dry bureaucratic decisions that led to her murder – he unearthed the family's entire paper trail from the time of their arrival in Norway to the time of their deportation. Their presence was woven through Norwegian census bureaus and hospitals, through schools and tax authorities, the financial official markers that indicated their slow but steady increase in prosperity, the rooms they lived in, the lives they led in material form. He strove to find those who could breathe life into the statistics. Yet he could not find many who still held distinct memories of Kathe, nor many of her words.

Despite these lacunae, Søbye's meticulous research draws a careful portrait of a girl whose life was always bound by her religious difference. The lack of sources, too, becomes a part of the story. What Søbye finds are the endless small machinations of persecution.

What he wanted were answers to the anodyne as well as the profound. How could this happen? Why her? Why did she not try to run? And if she had – where could she have gone? Who might have taken her in?

***

It is not strange that the search for Kathe was so difficult. The collaboration of the Quisling leadership, and of part of the police force itself, was impossible to celebrate, post-war. And so the stories were not told.

That Norway did not immediately address this past is also not all that peculiar. The early post-war period, as Søbye points out, was not marked by soul-searching. The despoiling of the Jews, carefully laid out in this book, was done methodically, meticulously. The very few Jews who returned found their access to the material goods of their dead hard to access.

In 1997 the Norwegian Ministry of Justice issued a white paper acknowledging a moral, and monetary, debt to the Jews. "The economic liquidation of the group as a whole was unique, and the organized arrest, deportation and physical destruction of the Jews was genocide. Since the aim was to completely destroy the Jewish group in Norway, the economic and physical liquidation must be regarded as two parts of the same crime," the ministers wrote. The liquidation of Jewish property, which had begun with Quisling's edict in October 1942, had been accompanied by a second, financially crushing, insult: taxes on that property had continued to accrue, even after the owners were divested of their real estate, jewelry, and other worldly possessions. But worse: the taxes piled up even after the owners were long dead. After the war, survivors were hit with back taxes for property the state had long-ago confiscated.

In that white paper, Norway announced reparations for that injustice as the millennium drew to a close. The money was to be spent to ensure the "preservation of Jewish culture and the future of the Jewish community in Norway."8

***

There are, among a large handful of writers alive today, a few of us who find ourselves obsessed with these stories. Often it is because of a personal access point to the history. We are Jews, and thus descendants of victims or survivors, and we find ourselves driven to understand stories of survival, or of destruction. This is my case. My grandfather

8   https://www.regjeringen.no/en/dokumenter/white_paper_no_82_1997-98/id201553/

fled Vienna in 1938. Or perhaps we are from the country which per-petrated the crime, and thus we search for what our ancestors did or did not do.

Espen Søbye falls into neither camp. He was, instead, born in 1954 to parents who were adolescents during the war, under occupa-tion. But from his parents he learned a bit about how they observed that dark period for the Jews of his country.

While in class one day, Søbye's mother – then a teenager – wit-nessed the arrest of a girl named Liv Marcus, a schoolmate. Marcus and her sister were ripped out of school in front of the horrified eyes of her fellow students in the town of Hamar. Søbye's mother pre-served the girl's belongings – the schoolbooks she placed upon her desk at her arrest, a few articles of clothing – and put them into a box. After the war, she returned this paltry collection to the girl's brother. He had managed to escape to Sweden. His sister was not so lucky. She, like so many others, was murdered upon arrival in Auschwitz.

In conversation Søbye elaborates further on what drew him to this work. "Nobody is only a victim," he explains. "When I came across the form Kathe Lasnik filled in and I started the research, the only thing that had survived about Kathe was that she was a victim of the Holocaust. The archives, the monuments, and even the memory of the girls she went to school with – they didn't remember much else other than that she was deported. It seemed that when a person was deported and killed in Auschwitz, that event erased every other event in the person's life.

"This, however, was what the fascists hoped for – that no trace, no memory of these people should bear witness to their lives. My inten-tion, even if this was not so clear to me when I started working on the book, was to try to reconstruct the daily life of Kathe Lasnik by telling her life story, trivial things from her daily life; by doing this I believed that it was still possible to resist the Final Solution and the fascist attempt to murder all European Jews."

Søbye insists it was "impossible" to fulfill his goals. He believes that his very late act of what he calls resistance failed. He worries that the very lack of sources themselves shows that, even this small resistance failed Kathe.

But I disagree with Søbye. This book, even belatedly, is an essential act of resistance that is both valiant and vital.

1

File 84/1 Is Empty

I WOULD NEVER have come across Kathe Lasnik, were it not for an e-mail from a colleague who worked at the International Criminal Court in The Hague. My colleague, it turned out, had been contacted by William Seltzer of Fordham University, who was investigating the role that statistics had played in the identification, isolation, and arrest of Jews during World War II. I had been asked to comment on the section that he had written about Norway.

Even though I worked at Statistics Norway (formerly Central Bureau of Statistics), the country's official bureau of statistics, I had no clue how statistics related to the persecution of Jews that took place in Norway. I was further chagrined to discover that William Seltzer's request could not be satisfied by the historical accounts. A few months after I had sent off my woefully incomplete comments, I was asked to speak at the 21st Nordic Conference on Statistics. And so that is what I chose for my subject: the role that statistics had played in the deportation of Jews from Norway in the fall of 1942.

My research into the matter required a trip to the National Archives, which is located in a gloomy spruce grove off the Sognsvann subway line on Oslo's west side. For a start, I delved into the archives of the Ministry of the Police from 1940-1945. There I found a whole bundle of forms, 1,419 in total, that Jews were required to fill out in triplicate before turning them in to their local police office. The forms were the brainchild of a 1942 initiative on the part of the National Unification Party's[1] Statistics Office. Randomly flipping through the stacks, I noticed that some had been filled out with a typewriter, others with a trembling elderly hand, and still others with a child's serious lettering. Furthermore, most of the forms had been filled out at the beginning of 1942.

Then I found Kathe Lasnik's form. Born October 13, 1927, she was a high school student, and I was struck by the fact that she had turned in her form much later than the others had – namely, on November 16, 1942, only fourteen days before she was sent to the gas chambers at Auschwitz. Why had she waited so long to fill out the form? Could she perhaps have avoided deportation if she had simply neglected to do it?

One of the questions the form asked was: "When did you come to Norway?" Kathe Lasnik answered: "I've always been in Norway." Why had she answered the question in exactly that way? Subsequent questions about birthplace and place of residence revealed that she had always lived in Norway; in answer to the question about nationality, she wrote: "Norwegian." Maybe Kathe Lasnik was unwilling to take any chances, I thought, and that is why she wrote, "I've always been in Norway." By the time she filled out the "Questionnaire for Jews in Norway," Jewish men were being arrested, and their shops and assets were being seized. Maybe she wrote "I've always been in Norway" because she thought that those words would protect her. "I've always been in Norway" was a kind of plea: I'm one of you; you wouldn't hurt me, would you? As it turned out, however, that is exactly what they did.

I ordered a copy of her form, even though I did not need it for my talk, and I put it in the binder with my other articles and archive material. The talk was written and delivered, and was later published under the title "Persecution of Jews During the Second World War: A Dark Chapter in the History of Statistics?".[2] Much of what I discovered in the course of my research was also useful to William Seltzer when he wrote his article.[3] And that was that. I was done with the war.

Every now and then, however, I would take the binder off the shelf and have a look at the form the fifteen-year-old girl had filled out on

November 16, 1942. One time, I even picked up the phone book – but no, there were no Lasniks left, not in Oslo, not in Norway.

Nonetheless, I finally found her in Our Fallen, a memorial publication in four red volumes issued by the Norwegian government: "LASNIK, KATHE RITA, high school student, Oslo. Born October 13, 1927 in Oslo, daughter of Elias Lasnik b. 1887 in Vilna and Dora b. Meszansky, b. 1888 ibidem. Arrested during the persecution of the Jews in Norway and sent to Germany on November 26, 1942, along with her parents and a sister. Upon arrival in Auschwitz in December of that year, she was immediately sent to the gas chamber."[4] There was a corresponding entry for her mother and father, and also for her sister, Anna Lasnik, who was born in 1911.

I also found her name on the bronze relief memorial at Fagerborg School in Oslo, which is dedicated to fallen students. Beneath her portrait are the words: "KATHE RITA LASNICK (daughter of master tinsmith Elias Lasnick and Dora Meszansky) born October 13, 1927 Oslo, student at Fagerborg School during the war. During the fall of 1942, she was arrested and deported to Germany. She was then sent to Poland, where her life was soon ended in the gas chambers at Auschwitz (Oswiecim)." The text beneath this picture is repeated in a booklet entitled "These Fagerborg School Students Gave Their Lives during the War."[5]

Another place Kathe Lasnik's name can be found is on the memorial at the Jewish Cemetery that lists the 620 Jews from the Oslo area who were killed during the war. However, the memorials and cenotaphs do not really contain a lot of information. All they do is tie her to the extermination. Is that, however, the only significant thing that happened in her life? I thought it was terrible that Kathe Lasnik was only remembered because she had been a victim. Was there perhaps someone out there who could remember her for something more?

I petitioned the National Archives for access to Kathe Lasnik's file from the Reparations Office for Confiscated Assets. This office, which was established on May 15, 1945, had inherited the archives from the Liquidation Board for Confiscated Jewish Property established by the Ministry of the Interior on October 26, 1942. According to page 293 of the National Archives' handbook, there should be an index card and folder for every individual whose possessions were entirely or partially confiscated.[6]

It was sometime around the end of March 2000 that I heard from the National Archives, which informed me that I had been granted access to box 995, file 84/1. While I was riding the Sognsvann subway line, I wondered what I would find in the file. What could one possibly seize from a child? A backpack full of schoolbooks, skis and ice skates, maybe a bike, a poetry journal, or a diary? I tried to imagine the men from the Liquidation Board tramping around the deported family's apartment, entering Kathe Lasnik's bedroom, moistening their pencils, and writing: a backpack full of schoolbooks, a shelf of children's books, a scrapbook, a bicycle. Or did folder 84/1 contain documents like a birth certificate, vaccination records, report cards, her elementary school diploma, her identification card, and maybe a death certificate?

An archivist retrieved the file from storage and brought it to the reading room where I had been asked to wait. File 84/1 was empty. There was a cover with her name, a number, and nothing more. And I was struck with a sudden impulse: Find out everything you can about Kathe Lasnik.

The file on her father, Elias Lasnik, contained documents showing that Elias and Dora Lasnik were the parents of not just two, but four daughters. There was a Jenny Lasnik, born in 1909, and an Elise Lasnik, born in 1913, in addition to Anna Lasnik, born in 1911, and Kathe Lasnik, who was born long after the others, in 1927. I also discovered that Jenny Lasnik had married Leopold Bermann in 1937 and that Elise Lasnik had married Julius Bassist in 1942.

Both of Kathe Lasnik's married sisters had fled to Sweden in the fall of 1942. Their husbands were long dead, but both sisters were still alive. Jenny Bermann had moved to Boston in 1954, while Elise Bassist had resided in Kfar Saba, a small town just north of Tel Aviv, since 1994.

In March 2001, I traveled to Tel Aviv to talk to Elise Bassist. I brought with me ten cans of Stabburet's mackerel in tomato sauce and weekly magazines containing royal gossip. That was all Elise Bassist wanted from Norway. One day I showed up with flowers, and while we laid them out on the small kitchen counter, she said that it had always been Julius Bassist, her husband, who had arranged the flowers, trimming the stalks and putting them into a vase.

Elise Bassist also told me about her escape from Norway to Sweden and what she had heard after the war regarding her family's arrest. A police officer had tried to save Kathe Lasnik's life. He had asked her if she had anyone to whom she wanted to say goodbye, just to give her a chance to flee. However, the family whose doorbell she had rung had not understood that. It would have been so easy for her to escape, too, because their apartment happened to have a back door, which opened onto a staircase leading down to the yard. She could have gone through the apartment, down that second set of stairs, and out the door. I did not say it aloud, but I wondered, did she have anywhere to go?

Instead, I talked about the fantastic skiing conditions we had experienced in Nordmarka outside the city before I left Oslo, and I rambled on about blue skies, Blue Swix ski wax, green Norway spruce trees, white snow, and dripping icicles. Before the war, she said, they had started their ski outings at the front door of their apartment building on Hertzbergs gate,[7] and had skied through the undeveloped areas in the districts of Marienlyst, Blindern, and Gaustad, and then out to Sognsvann Lake. Elise Bassist was living in a small apartment in a senior housing facility with a reception area and a cafeteria. A picture on one wall of her apartment showed a birch clinging to a hill next to a body of water, and she told me that in the summers they had always taken a trip to the countryside; her little sister had never needed to go to summer camp. They had rented places in Nesodden, and even farther out on the Oslofjord, in Asker and Sætre. After the war, she and her husband had even bought themselves a cabin on Glennestrand in Bunnefjorden. Her father, Elias Lasnik, had always been the one to insist that the family move to the countryside during the summer. He worked in the city, but he would visit them on weekends.

In February 2002, almost a year later, I went to see Jenny Bermann in Boston. "We shouldn't have a world that makes telling stories like this necessary," she repeated many times. Jenny Bermann was no longer very good at remembering details, but she pronounced her little sister's name with a deep, long e-sound. She had learned to speak Norwegian in Grünerløkka, Oslo, before the First World War, but her parents had mostly spoken Yiddish. It had not been possible for her to contact the rest of her family while she was in hiding with her son, waiting to be transported to Sweden. She had been too afraid to call.

By chance, my hotel was located just a few minutes' walk from her hospital room at St. Elizabeth's Medical Center. I had brought a few documents from the war and we looked at these together. The staff even gave us a room where we could be alone and I wheeled Jenny Bermann there. Despite how difficult it was for her to remember things, I wanted to make it clear that I was trying to find out as much as possible about Kathe Lasnik. I did not ask for Jenny Bermann's and Elise Bassist's permission to do so. I was not willing to let them decide whether it was right to follow my impulse. This was my task and my responsibility, but I was very glad that they were both willing to help me.

Elise Bassist told me that her parents, Elias Lasnik and Dora Meszansky, came to Norway as refugees in 1908. They immigrated to the country before they were married and had only two duvets and 25 kroner to their name. They came from the place known to Russians and Jews as Vilna, to Poles as Wilno, and to Lithuanians as Vilnius.

After my visits to Jenny Bermann and Elise Bassist, the only contemporaneous documents I had of Kathe Lasnik and her family were a few photographs. Papers, certificates, diplomas, letters and various other forms of documentation – all were missing. After all, there was not much they could take with them when they fled to Sweden; when they returned after the war, everything was gone. Kathe Lasnik's sisters answered my questions, but the questions themselves were hard to ask. I realized that it was painful for them to recall their little sister and the time they had spent together. Indeed, I had not been prepared that the quest to find out as much as possible about Kathe Lasnik would be paralyzed by the pain of memory.

It turned out that the most important source of information about the Lasnik family was Oslo's annual census. There was a form for every household in the city, and all inhabitants were required to provide their name, occupation, place of employment, and the time and place of their birth. Tax forms also contained information on the annual income of Kathe Lasnik's father and older sisters.

So what other sources of information exist about a girl who grew up in Oslo between the two World Wars? Kathe Lasnik attended three different schools. Møllergata School still kept the attendance records for the class to which she belonged from August 1934 until Christmas break 1938. She took her elementary school exams at Majorstua School, and the evaluation records for class 7C from June 1941 are also extant. Fagerborg Middle School retains exam records for class 1D and the fall term exam records for class 2D from 1942.

In elementary school, Kathe Lasnik was part of an all-girls class. To find out the names, birth dates, and addresses of the girls in her class at Møllergata School, I sent a request to the Special Registry at Sør-Hedmark's County Tax Office, which handles this type of inquiry. After a few days, I received a list of married names and addresses of the girls. Four were dead, and the Special Registry could not locate six of the girls. Of the sixteen who were left, fourteen of them lived in or around the Oslo area, one lived in Drammen, and one lived in Sandefjord.

All of them remembered Kathe Lasnik. She had dark, wavy hair, brown eyes, and she was not a Christian. Everyone knew that she was Jewish. However, none of them thought that she was ever teased or singled out for it. Many of them knew where she had lived and a few of them had even been to her apartment. However, one girl said: "We weren't really eager to include her in the circle; she went home right after school. I didn't even know where she lived."

I further learned that the members of class 7C, who took their elementary school exam at Majorstua School in 1941, regularly got together. Indeed, the summer of 2001 would mark their 60th anniversary. Lillan Grosch, who was organizing the festivities, had a list with all the girls' married names on it. Kathe Lasnik and three others were dead, three had emigrated from Norway to the USA, and one had moved to Israel.

Lillan Grosch told me that when the girls from 7C came together again for the first time in 1946, they remembered Kathe Lasnik with a minute of silence. At the upcoming anniversary celebration, she would tell everyone what I was doing and ask anyone who might remember something to contact me. She also made a few phone calls, but she told me that "recollection" in general was not good. Nonetheless, in talking to Kathe Lasnik's school friends from Majorstua School, I found out about the boys who had lived near Hertzbergs gate in Fagerborg. They had also been Kathe Lasnik's classmates.

At Fagerborg Middle School, namely, the class was co-ed. A couple of the boys even recalled a farewell letter that Kathe Lasnik supposedly wrote the morning she was arrested. Apparently, the letter was read aloud by Hans Christian Norløff, a teacher at the school. When he read the letter, tears stood in his eyes, and the girls cried. "Thanks for everything. You won't see me again. Last night we were arrested."

Not everyone in the class remembers the letter and I myself do not know what to believe. Once again, I was confronted with something I had not foreseen when I started my investigation. Why was it so difficult to remember Kathe Lasnik? Recalling her seemed difficult, even for her friends. Had the extermination wiped out all other memories? That was certainly what it seemed like.

How can we discover whether Kathe Lasnik really wrote that farewell letter? Did Mr. Norløff take the letter home after he had read it aloud? He taught at Fagerborg from 1935 to 1949. According to the catalogue at the University of Oslo Library, he graduated with a math degree in 1920 and wrote a thesis entitled On the Function $f(z) = A \ln(z+1) + B \ln(z-1)$. He could have been born around 1895 and is probably long dead. If his children still have his papers, could it be that Kathe Lasnik's farewell letter is among them?

There is an article entitled "Statistical Overview of Wartime Deaths 1940-1945,"[8] by demographer Julie Backer. In the article, Julie Backer proceeds to account for all the Norwegian deaths brought about by Hitler Germany's wartime operations and the Nazi occupation. The problem is, most of the prisoners who died in Auschwitz were never declared dead by a physician or any civil authorities. As a result, when Julie Backer put together her statistical account after the war, she relied on survivor testimony. A cardboard box located in Statistics Norway's basement archive contains all the supporting material for her tables – namely, 10,262 death reports that are wrapped in brown paper and bound together according to category: soldiers on the battlefield, sailors, civilians, Jews, and so forth. I opened the packet marked "Jews" and found a form with Kathe Lasnik's name on it. As it turns out, the nearest thing she has to a death certificate was located in the building at Kongensgate 6 where I worked. The "certificate" itself was about as big as an envelope. Indeed, it was nothing more than a stenciled form that, filled out in pencil, recorded her date of birth, place of residence, and date of death.

Kathe Lasnik's date of death is given as December 1, 1942. That is the date on which the Jews arrested in Oslo on November 26 arrived at Auschwitz. A member of the German secret service accordingly reported that a train with 532 Norwegian Jews arrived just before 11:00 p.m. The commandant of Auschwitz II (Birkenau) then signed for the delivery on the list of names accompanying the transport.[9] After they arrived, 186 men between 15 and 50 years old were immediately sent to work and were given prisoner numbers 79,064 to 79,249.[10] All the older men, women, and children were carted away in cargo trucks.

2

From Vilna to Kristiania

KATHE LASNIK'S PARENTS filled out the "Questionnaire for Jews in Norway" in March of 1942. In answer to the question "When did you come to Norway?" they wrote: "June 20, 1908."[12] An employee of Kristiania's municipal registry, which was established on April 7, 1909, wrote "08 aug" under the heading: "Date moved to Kristiania[11] (Norway)."[13] Elias Lasnik and Dora Meszansky, who left Russia because the former had been drafted into the military, arrived in Norway the summer of 1908.[14] But neither a yellowed summons drafted in Cyrillic script, nor any note written in Hebraically-lettered Yiddish, asking her to come with him, is still in existence today. They were both young when they fled. Elias was born in 1887, Dora in 1888. Dodging military duty was punishable by death or by lifelong exile.

Elias Lasnik and Dora Meszansky were not the only Jews to flee Russia. In 1881, Jewish emigration from Russia to the big cities of Vienna, Berlin, London, Antwerp, Paris, Johannesburg, Buenos Aires, Melbourne, and New York began in earnest.[15] Most emigrants, however, went to New York, and by 1908 over 100,000 Jews from Russia, Austria-Hungary, and Romania had settled there.[16] The Jewish concentration was by far the largest on Manhattan's Lower East Side.[17]

It is easy to understand why so many Jews chose to become émigrés. At the time, there were six million Jews living in a belt called "Yiddishland" that stretched from Odessa on the Black Sea to Riga and Danzig on the Baltic Sea.[18] Jews were, furthermore, only allowed to settle in certain locations and a number of laws restricted their rights.[19]

Sir Henry Beaumont at the British Embassy in St. Petersburg traveled around "Yiddishland" in the summer of 1905. The worst poverty he encountered was in Vilna, the birthplace of Elias Lasnik and Dora Meszansky. The diplomat was further informed by the town's Jewish Aid Committee that about a third of the Jewish families in the area were considered destitute. Indeed, with its "narrow streets, overcrowded houses, its dirt and unsavory smells," Vilna contained "so much misery" that the diplomat could only compare it with "the worst slums of Whitechapel."[20] According to Beaumont, moreover, overpopulation and ruinous economic competition were to blame for the misery he saw around him.

Elias Lasnik and Dora Meszansky took the train to Germany and from there to Kristiania.[21] At the time, the city had 235,000 inhabitants and was only a bit larger than Vilna. It is no easy task to find out exactly what Vilna's population was before World War I. However, according to a nearly century-old edition of the Danish Encyclopedia, *Salmonsens konversationsleksikon*, half of the inhabitants were Polish, forty percent were Jews, and the rest were Russians, Lithuanians and Germans.[22]

As it turned out, Elias Lasnik already had a number of relatives in Kristiania, as well as a brother and a sister in New York.[23] Perhaps Elias and Dora, like plenty of people before them, had only planned on staying in Norway until they had enough money to travel across the ocean.

Elias Lasnik's grandfather had been married three times, and five of his children – four daughters and a son – were living in Kristiania in 1908.[24] They were all married and among them they had seventeen children. The oldest sibling had settled in Kristiania in 1886 – that is, before Elias Lasnik and Dora Meszansky were even born. Elias Lasnik's relatives spoke both Norwegian and Yiddish and so could help the young couple, who only spoke Yiddish, a little Russian and Hebrew, get adjusted.[25]

One of Elias Lasnik's aunts was married to a "fruit vendor"[26] and lived at Akersgaten 73. Another had married a man who had begun as a shoemaker, but who was also running a fruit and tobacco shop in 1908.[27] This couple lived at Thorvald Meyers gate 26. Elias Lasnik's uncle on his mother's side had been a "cigarette factory worker"[28] before he opened a glassware shop, the Hamburger Bazaar, at Brogaten 5. Together with his family, he lived at Thorvald Meyers gate 36.[29] The third aunt was married to a carpenter and lived at Seilduksgaten 9,[30] while the fourth ran a shop, Føniks Gentlemen's Outfitters, together with her husband and lived in an annex at Eilert Sundts gate 53.[31]

When Isak Leimann, Elias Lasnik's uncle, filled out the form for Kristiania's annual municipal census on February 1, 1909, he added that unmarried tinsmith Elias Lasnik also lived in the apartment at Thorvald Meyers gate 26.[32] As a result, this form is the first written evidence, at least in Norway, of what was to become the Lasnik family.

None of Elias Lasnik's other relatives reported that Dora Meszansky was staying with them. They might have merely forgotten to mention her. In 1908, anyone could settle in Norway, so they had nothing to conceal. On the contrary, there was a "monetary fine" levied for not listing everyone in a given apartment.[33]

Indeed, according to *Fremmedloven*, the legislation regulating immigration to the country, Elias Lasnik and Dora Meszansky could establish "permanent residence and seek employment" without Norwegian citizenship. However, first they had to "present themselves to the local chief of police," who would then examine all "identification papers, if these [were] available." If it appeared likely that the individual could "find legal employment in the country," the person in question was given a "residency booklet."[34] This booklet then had to be presented every time the individual changed jobs or location, or if there was a change in the person's civil status. Although this booklet gave individuals the right to stay in the country, at least as long as they had work and could provide for themselves and all dependents, it did not give the bearer civil rights.

3

Apprentice Tinsmith and Tobacco Factory Worker

ELIAS LASNIK FOUND a job at the Norwegian Metalware Factory, a tinsmith's workshop located behind Waldemar Thranes gate 63,[35] while Dora Meszansky began work at Moritz Glott's Cigar & Cigarette Factory, which was located at Storgaten 24.[36]

Master tinsmith A. Halvorsen owned the metalware factory. At the time Elias Lasnik began his apprenticeship, Kristiania had 72 different tinsmith shops and a total of 203 workers.[37] During the summer of 1908, the apprentice tinsmiths actually went on a three-month strike in order to get their workday reduced from ten to nine-and-a-half hours and their minimum wage increased from 35 to 40 øre an hour.[38]

The tobacco industry in Kristiania was also important. There were 13 tobacco factories in the city alone. The eastern part of Norway had 20 more factories, which employed 325 men, 572 women, and 248 boys and girls under the age of eighteen.[39] Each of the 90 women around Dora's age earned 22 Norwegian øre an hour, or about 11 kroner for a 50-hour work week.

The couple from Vilna belonged to the lowest income class. At the same time, plenty of people managed to scrape by on what they earned,[40] and by February 1909 they had found an apartment and could get married.

The marriage ceremony took place on March 4, 1909, in the Jewish Congregation at Brogaten 5. Two of the witnesses to the ceremony were Elias Lasnik's uncles, Isak Leimann and Samuel Kazerginski, and the third was the religion instructor Nochem Salomon Meirowitz.[41] The bridal pair presented their vaccination records; the bride and groom declared that they were not "related to each other." The groom said that he was the son of a broom maker, while the bride was the daughter of a carpenter. And with that tinsmith Elias Kalman Lasnik "from the Jewish community of Vilna in Russia" was married to tobacco factory worker Dora Meszansky from the same community.[42]

Elias Lasnik had been accepted into the Jewish Congregation the day before the wedding.[43] In fact, he was the last person to be accepted into the congregation, which had been founded in 1893.[44] The wedding was also the last service to be held before the synagogue either closed its doors or ceased its operations.[45]

In 1909, there were a number of Jewish congregations in Kristiania. Since the ban against Jewish immigration had been lifted in 1851, many Jews coming to Norway were from Denmark and Germany. These individuals, together with the Russian Jews who had already been in the country a long time, controlled the Mosaic Religious Community. At the same time, because the number of Jews coming to Kristiania from Russia was comparatively greater than the number of Jews who were already established there, conflicts between the two groups arose. On the one hand, the newly arrived Russian and Polish Jews were displeased by the fact that the already-established group was in control. On the other hand, the Jews who had been in Norway for a long time defended their position by emphasizing the fact that the newly arrived Jews did not know the language and, therefore, could not participate in decision-making or voting.[46] As a result of these conflicts, a number of Jewish families did not belong to any congregation. Of course, there were also families who could not afford to pay the membership fee.[47] After the Jewish Congregation closed, Elias and Dora Lasnik did not join another religious community until 1921.

The newly married couple first settled at Grünersgate 5,[48] but on November 1, 1909, they moved to the second floor of a backyard building at Markveien 28.[49] Nochem Salomon Meirowitz, who had been a witness at their wedding, lived at the same address. Their apartment, which cost 15 kroner a month, consisted of a living room and a kitchen.[50] Nine months to the day after the wedding, on December

4, 1909, Dora Lasnik gave birth to her daughter Jenny. Not long after the birth, Dora returned to her job at the tobacco factory, taking the infant with her.[51]

On April 7, 1909, the Kristiania population registry drew up a registration card for Elias Lasnik and his family.[52] The card would be updated each year with census information. Accordingly, Elias Lasnik first filled out the form for his apartment in February 1910. By then, the apprentice tinsmith from Vilna had learned so much Norwegian that he made very few mistakes. Indeed, his letters are like those a child makes just after first learning to write. He gave his own name as Elias Lasnik, but for his wife and child he wrote "Dure" and "Ini," their names in Yiddish. For his wife and himself he put Russia as the birthplace; for his child, Kristiania. In the columns reserved for profession and employment, he wrote tinsmith.[53]

In 1890, there were only 136 Jews living in Kristiania; by 1910, there were 688. Most of these were Russian immigrants. Of these, 583 settled in the parishes of Paulus, Jakob, and Trefoldighet, which are all located on the city's east side. By comparison, only 40 Jews lived in the parishes of Frogner, Uranienborg, and Fagerborg on the city's west side.[54] New York City, on the other hand, had a Jewish population of 2.5 million, and boasted numerous Jewish newspapers, as well as 20 theaters that featured plays in Yiddish.[55] In Kristiania, the Russian Jews met every Sunday at Olav Ryes Square to speak Yiddish.[56]

Nonetheless, Supreme Court lawyer Eivind Saxland published an anti-Semitic pamphlet in 1910, which argued that far too many Jews were coming to Norway. In answer, the critic Georg Brandes, a leading Scandinavian intellectual and cultural figure, ridiculed both the pamphlet and the whole Jewish debate in Norway in general: Saxlund, namely, "warned poor Norway about the terrible oppression that will be unleashed by the one-and-a-half Jews who were finally allowed to enter the country in the nineteenth century."[57] That same year, the Norwegian newspaper *Aftenposten* wrote an article about the English police, who were convinced that "Scandinavian countries house a large number of Russian revolutionaries and other Russian fugitives, who are dangerous to public security." Deciding to investigate the matter further, reporters from the newspaper took to the streets.

The resulting news story hit the stands on January 24, 1911. According to the paper, Copenhagen and Stockholm had "significant Russian communities, particularly Copenhagen, where large flocks of Russian and Polish Jews are gathered." At the same time, the police observed that this was not the case in Kristiania: "Not too many Russians have come here. In total, fifty [individuals] have registered their arrival in Kristiania. Almost all of them are Jews who have come from the Baltics and Poland." Indeed, it seemed that the number "of true Russians is in drastic decline. One gets the impression, however, that emigrants coming from Russia often neglect to register themselves. And these are presumably the sort of the people who are not exactly on the up and up."

Did Kristiania's police, *Aftenposten* asked, have much trouble with Russian Jews? "In terms of real Russians, I cannot remember ever having much to complain about. The only ones who ever cause any trouble are the Jewish peddlers who carry out unlawful business in more rural areas. On the whole, though, I have to say that Russian immigrants are just as polite and well-mannered as other immigrants." The police further told the newspaper that "[a]lmost all [the Russian immigrants] are Jews and either craftsmen or merchants. It is especially commerce that they conduct in the city. They run fruit shops, 10-øre bazaars and small tobacco shops. We have several hundred of these types of Russians; however, they lead a quiet and peaceful existence. On the rare occasion that the police hear anything from them, it is because they have had a falling out amongst themselves. They do not have much to do with Norwegians in general, since they keep to themselves and interact mostly with each other. They are poor but decent folk, who are sincerely happy to be in this country, and they do not want to do anything that would bring them into conflict with the police and cause them to be thrown out."

Aftenposten then further described the aforementioned Jews who came from Russia and did business in Norway. "Most of these immigrants live in the area around Calmeyergaden and Hausmansgaden, as well as in Enerhaugen. Many of them are quite uneducated. Most of them can barely read. Nonetheless, even though they are poor, they are an energetic and hard-working people." It was a bit different, however, with the immigrants who "only recently arrived in the country and cannot speak the language," since most of them led "a miserable and poor life. They struggle to support themselves from day to day by peddling." However, these people were also content and were "sincerely glad to have found refuge here in this country, where they can live peacefully." One thing, however, was not quite as it should be. "The newly immigrated Jewish families from Russia and Poland do not do much to improve the appearance of the area in which they live. In addition, they are often unwashed and their food is not always well prepared. It is only after they have been here a while that they learn the country's habits and begin to live a healthier life."[58]

A week later, K. W. from the newspaper *Dagbladet* took a walk "in the area around Bernt Ankers gate, Calmeyergaten and Osterhausgaten." He wanted, namely, to find out if there was really a ghetto down there. "The first thing I saw in Calmeyergaten was an ashen-faced, pale, blue-eyed Norwegian around seven or eight years old; he was tall and skinny and slouching and had a cap turned up over his ears. He was the spitting image of one of those chlorophyll-poor shoots that potatoes send out in the spring when they are down in a black cellar. When he had passed me by, I heard his weak voice scornfully mutter: 'the Jew, Israel.'

"I looked back and discovered a small, strong, compact boy with dark hair and dark, heavy brown eyes. He hastily walked away with a milk pail in his hand.

"I turned around and asked the beanstalk why he had said that to the little boy, but he just smiled and shyly ducked into the same door where the little brown-eyed boy had disappeared.

"Since I wanted to have a closer look at the building, I followed him. And it was no cheerful sight that met me. The entryway wallpaper was so dirty that it was only here and there that you could still see colors and decorations. Most of the space in the narrow, shadowy courtyard was taken up by sundry kinds of debris. There were large crates packed with rusty coal scuttles and tin pails, all full of holes, heaps of rags, big bundles of feathers, and other rubbish.

"It seemed like the building's inhabitants, however, did have some business sense. I wandered up the stairs, which were richly decorated with eye-catching placards in every color. 'Huge fire and liquidation sale,' '500 women's underskirts sold at bargain prices today,' 'A large quantity of soiled hose sold cheap,' etc. Several Jewish stereotypes were also visible out on the street. It gave you the feeling that you really were in some kind of miniature Ghetto. I asked one of the polite, obliging Jews where the synagogue's religious leader could be found, and was directed to the merchant S. I. Feinberg on Torvgaten, where I was heartily welcomed.

"In response to my question about whether or not there was a so-called Jewish quarter down around Calmeyergaten, he answered:

"'Absolutely not. That is just something *Aftenposten* claimed. Of course, there are not as many well-off Jewish families down there, but there is no way it can be called a Jewish quarter. Jews are spread across the city. There are probably as many on the west side as there are on the east.

"'The reason that someone compared it to a Jewish quarter is that the synagogue is here in the area, on Østre Elvebakken. When services are held, a large number of Jews are often assembled, and from that *Aftenposten* suddenly concludes that all Jews live in that area.'

"How many Jews live in the city?

"'There are about 500 souls.'

"Is the number steadily rising?

"'In the last year, there has not been any significant increase. Since the bloodbath in Russia a couple of years ago, not many Jews have traveled here to this country. But the Jews who are here are happy and have tried hard to get to know their new homeland. The younger Jews thirst after knowledge. Many of them have qualified for the university. Jews are represented in the [military] officer profession, the teaching profession, the legal profession, and so on. It is not true that the Jews here in the city are mainly businessmen. It is possible that these are the most visible, but their numbers are small compared to those who earn their living in other ways. Here in the city one can find Jews in just about every line of work.'

"I told him about the aforementioned street episode and asked him if Jews in general noticed any real racism here and if children were the target of insults at school.

"'It is not something we hear about often. Jewish children do fine at school and get along well with their classmates, both in elementary school and beyond. Every once in a while, street urchins say something abusive. Indeed, if the situation everywhere else were as good as in the schools, all would be good and well.'

"Have you noticed, then, any anti-Semitic movement here in the city?

"'Have you noticed that whenever a Jew does something immoral, the fact that he's Jewish gets plenty of attention? And have you noticed that when a Jew does something worthy, the fact that he's Jewish is never mentioned? For example, when it was announced the other day that old Volmann had left a large sum of money to well-deserving charities here in the city, no one bothered to mention that he was Jewish.'"[59]

4

Wilses Gate 6

THE 152 MEMBERS of the Apprentice Tinsmiths' Association in Kristiania went on strike nearly every time their wage agreement was up for renewal.[60] There were also conflicts at Glott's Cigar & Cigarette Factory. The tobacco factory workers wanted a pay increase from 1.75 kroner to 2.75 kroner for every 1,000 cigarettes rolled with mouthpiece installed. Moritz Glott answered that the "fierce competition, especially on two-øre cigarettes," made it impossible to agree to what "the workers demanded." It was, in fact, "the American Trust Company" that created the problem, because it "delivers 1,200 cigarettes for the price of 1,000." If the government would put a stop to the dumping, Glott continued, it would be "a pleasure to meet my workers' demands."[61]

In 1911, Elias and Dora Lasnik together earned between 40 and 50 kroner per week. For the three people at Markveien 28, however, that was just fine. Nonetheless, when Halvorsen could not offer any apprentice positions during the winter, the situation got worse. And when Dora Lasnik gave birth to her second child on November 19, 1911, she could no longer work. Having two small children at the factory was not an option. The new baby's name was Anna Esther. At that time, Anna was the most common girl's name in Norway.[62] Though Elias and Dora Lasnik had given their child a popular Norwegian name, when it came time for Elias Lasnik to fill out the list of persons on the municipal census form, he once again wrote the female names in Yiddish, only this time with a different spelling: "Dura", "Jeni" and "Ane".[63]

In August 1912, Elias and Dora Lasnik and their two small girls moved to an apartment at Wilses gate 6, which was actually a store with a back room.[64] The plan was for Dora Lasnik to run a fruit store while she watched the children.[65] Elias Lasnik's uncles, Isak Leimann and Samuel Kazerginski, also ran fruit stores. The rent at the new Wilses gate apartment was 35 kroner a month, 20 kroner more than at Markveien.[66] However, rent was also the only business expense the couple had, since the wholesale suppliers were paid only after all the retail goods were sold.[67]

Wilses gate 6 was located in the parish of Trefoldighet on the west side of the Akerselva river vis-à-vis lower Grünerløkka. The building had running water, a gas line and cooking range, an electric doorbell and a portable toilet set into the cement floor of the hallway.[68] The block of well-built apartment buildings between Møllergata, Wilses gate, Deichmans gate and Christ Cemetery, which includes the building at Wilses gate 6, all date from the end of the nineteenth century and contrast sharply with the old and tumble-down wooden buildings around Hammersborg Torg.

The Lasniks' fruit store was located directly to the right of the front door and occupied 12 square meters. The back room was about the same size and had a little window overlooking the courtyard.[69] Abraham Josef Koritzinsky,[70] who was also a Russian immigrant, owned the building. After living for a few years in Karlstad, he had immigrated to Kristiania from Ratskij in 1885.[71] In 1912, the building had two other stores on the ground floor: an outlet selling "hardware and more" and a "notions shop." However, the fruit store was the only one that came with a family apartment,[72] as the back room was called.

According to the files at the National Population Register, Elias Lasnik had paid taxes since 1910,[73] but it was only during the 1913/14 fiscal year that he was officially registered at the tax office in Kristiania and paid taxes on an income of 1,200 kroner.[74] After the rent was paid 780 kroner remained, which meant that the family had 15 kroner a week to live on. The Lasniks' income placed them in the lowest income bracket, which was made up of 10 percent of working households earning between 1,200 and 1,500 kroner a year.[75] Kristiania's municipal statistics office, in fact, conducted a thorough survey of the average household in this income group. According to this survey, 700 kroner went for food, while 133 kroner went for clothes and footwear. After rent, electricity, fuel, and all other expenses were paid, 15 kroner remained for household expenses, and 8.22 kroner for "pleasure and entertainment."[76]

The Lasnik family's income level was low, that is, but not unusual. At the same time, not many families lived in the back room of a shop. When Dora Lasnik gave birth to another girl on December 31, 1913, the room became too cramped and the family moved to an apartment on the third floor, which had two rooms and a kitchen. However, it is not clear from either the files at the National Population Register or from the annual census if the family made the move before or after the new addition to the family. Whatever the case, it was impossible for Dora Lasnik to keep running the fruit store with three small girls too look after. The new baby's name was Elise, but when Elias Lasnik filled out the census form, he wrote "Lissa" in addition to "Jenni" and "Ana."[77]

The rent for the new third floor apartment was 35 kroner a month. Anna Mathilde Pedersen from Lier was the "maid,"[78] and in addition to her wages, she earned food and board. Other than that, a maid did not cost much, only about 3-4 kroner a week.[79] Nonetheless, Dora Lasnik did not enjoy help for long. Instead, the family was forced to rent out the room to Kristen Solheim, a warehouse worker from Gloppen, and Mikjel Skaalheim, a wagoner from Vikøy.[80]

Before World War I broke out, Norwegian newspapers described the hordes of Russian saw filers who were settling in Kristiania. Supposedly, these people represented a great danger to the country and Chief Johan Søhr of the Police Detective Bureau had no doubt that there were "saw filers whose mission both here and in Sweden is to spy and gather information that might be of military significance to Russia." Indeed, he knew of one saw filer in particular who had been a "Russian officer."[81] With the start of the World War, anxiety about the Russians reappeared. According to John Søhr, Great Britain was "sending entire shiploads of people, who came from Russia, Poland, or the Baltics," to Bergen. Many of these people were Jews, and the original plan was to send them to Russia. However, as the bureau chief complained, "due to the lack of regulation and supervision, far too many of these people were given the chance to settle here in the country, which, as a result, was seeing a huge increase in the number of undesirable individuals. Many of them," the chief continued, "have become troublesome and expensive. It has since proved impossible to get rid of them again."[82]

When war broke out on the continent, nearly all trade in Kristiania stopped. Things quickly picked up again, however, and during the first year of the war, Elias Lasnik's income rose and he paid taxes on 1,700 kroner.[83] In 1915/16 and 1916/17, he paid taxes on 1,500 kroner.[84] In the war's last year, he earned even more: 1,900 kroner. And when the economic boom of 1918/19 hit, creating favorable conditions for the building industry and for craftsmen in general, Elias Lasnik earned a total of 2,500 kroner. The following year, that sum rose to 3,900 kroner.[85]

Even though purchasing power had been reduced by inflation, the family managed to live more comfortably. Since they had more money to spend, Elias and Dora Lasnik even bought a piano for their oldest daughter, Jenny. Until then she had often sat and "played piano" on the kitchen table. One day, however, a shiny new Zeitter & Winkelmann appeared in the apartment. However, the piano was not just there for entertainment. The parents really believed that their oldest daughter could be a pianist one day, and so she began taking lessons.[86]

In the fall of 1920, all three Lasnik sisters entered Møllergata School in the first, third, and fifth grades. They all had long, dark hair, which they helped each other to brush every morning. Even though they lived right across the street from the school, they were often late for class because they had spent too much time on their hair.[87]

For ten years, Elias Lasnik had always listed his profession as "tin-smith" when he filled out the annual census form, and this is what he again wrote in February, 1920.[88] The Kristiania Address Book, further-more, lists him as a journeyman tinsmith, with "A. Halvorsen" written next to this in parentheses. This shows that he was still employed at the tinsmith workshop located at Waldemar Thranes gate 63.

In 1921, however, the date of the municipal census was changed from February 1 to December 1. This meant that when Elias Lasnik filled out the form again, nearly two years had passed. He still wrote "tinsmith" in the place reserved for "profession and employment," but he also added something important in parentheses: "self-employed."[89]

5

Declared Free

ELIAS LASNIK'S FIRST workshop was located in the David-Andersen building on Egertorvet Square, just behind Karl Johansgate 20.[90] Since he was not yet a master tinsmith, he could only take on small jobs, such as repair and maintenance work. Nonetheless, he made 5,000[91] kroner in his first year, more than he had ever earned while working for Halvorsen.

Since 1866, craftsmen had held the right to set up shop and conduct business accordingly. However, in 1895 the Norwegian parliament adopted a trade law that gave master craftsmen the power to "keep an eye on unlawful trade operations" and, furthermore, to administer a final apprenticeship exam, thereby determining who would bear the title of master.[92]

Anyone could practice a craft, that is, but without a master certificate it was unlawful for the individual in question "to use any help other than his wife and the children who live at home." At the same time, the craftsman "could use whatever help may be necessary for the completion of that part of his personal labor that does not require a craftsman's ability."[93]

Not only had Elias Lasnik been an apprentice tinsmith for twelve years, but he had also taken courses at the technical college on Elvebakken. As a result, he had long been preparing to earn his master certificate.[94] The final apprenticeship exam consisted of two parts, one practical and one theoretical. The practical part of the exam required the candidate to make a cover for a stove or a brass pot; though the theoretical part was primarily devoted to economic calculations, the candidate also had to prove that he had the knowledge necessary for a business license.[95]

Neither the National Archives nor the Oslo City Archives could tell me why Elias Lasnik did not achieve the rank of master tinsmith. At the Industry Office in the Ministry of Trade and Industry, I pored through folders full of complaints from apprentices who did not become craft guild members. However, I found no letter from Elias Lasnik. At this point, I turned to the Oslo Coppersmiths' and Tinsmiths' Guild, whose offices are at Haslevangen 45A. It took a while, however, before the archive was finally located in an iron case that had been stuffed into a closet along with other junk. The oldest governing body and member protocols dated from 1920. I was offered an office and there I sat with the large handwritten pages before me. I found Elias Lasnik's name almost immediately.

The context in which his name was mentioned happened to be a guild meeting that took place on Friday, November 20, 1920, when Foreman Henrik Robarth set out to explain "the matter with Lasnitz [sic] and Gorvitz."[96] However, it was not immediately clear from the records what the matter concerned. At the yearly meeting in December, the issue was again addressed, and the members were assured that "notification had been sent" and, furthermore, that the foreman himself had "repeatedly" gone to the police to give testimony.[97]

Although none of this shed any light on the issue, at least I had a new name: Gorvitz. As it turned out, there was now only one Gorvitz in Oslo: Moritz Gorvitz, a ninety-year-old tinsmith who knew exactly what the matter had been about. Moritz Gorvitz is the son of Adolf Gorvitz; his father is the individual mentioned together with Elias Lasnik in the report from 1920. Adolf Gorvitz, who was born in Libau in 1884, had worked in Germany and Denmark before coming to Kristiania in 1910. For many years, he had worked as an apprentice tinsmith at master tinsmith Walbye's workshop, which was located at Bredegaten 22.

Like Elias Lasnik, Adolf Gorvitz had prepared himself thoroughly for his master certificate. When the stove cover required by his final apprenticeship exam did not pass muster, he thought it was absolutely ridiculous. In fact, he dismissed the rejection outright and went into business for himself.[98] Moritz Gorvitz, who began working at his father's shop toward the end of the 1920s, remembered Elias Lasnik well.

I concluded that the same thing must have happened to Elias Lasnik – that is, his stove cover had not passed muster. Moritz Gorvitz told me that the masters had regularly accused the Eastern European Jewish tinsmiths of unlawful trade practices; there had been one more besides his father and Elias Lasnik, but Moritz Gorvitz could not recall the man's name.

As Moritz Gorvitz was showing me around his house, I realized that he could probably tell me all about the wartime tinsmithing industry. In a little living room off the study hung a picture, taken some time before the war, that showed Adolf Gorvitz, his wife, and their nine children. I do not know how it came about, but suddenly I was supposed to guess which person was Moritz Gorvitz. I got it on the third try. All six boys had started out working in their father's shop. Moritz Gorvitz also told me that, with the exception of one sister, his whole family had been deported to Germany during the war and murdered. He himself had been imprisoned at Berg internment camp near Tønsberg in Norway from the fall of 1942 until the end of the war. However, since he was married to a non-Jewish woman, he was never actually deported. One of his brothers had sent him a letter from Auschwitz; he tried to find it, but it was not where he thought he had put it.

Eventually, Guild Foreman Henrik Robarth's visit to the police bore fruit and Elias Lasnik was accused of violating a temporary regulation that concerned commodity trading and pricing.[99] In July 1920, Elias Lasnik had supposedly "used two men, where one would suffice" in the "completion of tinsmithing work for merchant Dæhlen's villa 'Vestvik' on Malmøen." A compensatory sum of 375.15 kroner was demanded for the infraction, although 303.87 kroner would "be considered enough."[100] Ultimately, however, the court decided that since Elias Lasnik had not actually paid his assistant, he had "earned a fair wage in this particular case" for the work he had performed.[101]

It is reasonable to suppose that Elias Lasnik traveled to Oslo's lay court, which was where the judgment was rendered on February 25, 1921. According to the description given in his residency booklet, he was 151 cm. tall, had an average build, an oval face, a healthy complexion, brown hair and brown eyes, but otherwise no striking features.[102] When Judge Anton Getz had finished reading through the indictment, the law, and the terms, he explained the courts' unanimous decision: "Elias Lasnik should be declared innocent of the prosecuting authority's accusations."[103]

The masters, of course, were forced to submit to the court's decision. Nonetheless, when their governing body again met in November 1921, it was reported that Lasnik had accepted the roofing job on Høyer-Ellefsen's new building. This time they complained that he had accepted too low a sum for the job and so the governing body decided "to thoroughly look into the matter."[104] At the members' meeting, a number of people also demanded that "the matter receive full attention."[105] However, a formal complaint was never filed.

The largest steady job Elias Lasnik ever received was the maintenance work on the National Telegraph building at Prinsens gate 20. During the winter, when it was too cold to work in his backyard workshop, he cleared the snow and ice off the telegraph building's roof. His wife and children were anxious for him when he was up on the icy roof and, indeed, one time he fell through a hole and came home bruised and battered.[106] Elias Lasnik worked hard and in 1921/22 he earned 5,900 kroner, the highest income on which he would ever be taxed.[107] In 1922/23 and 1923/24, when the market was down and times were bad, he also did well and paid taxes on 4,800 kroner and 5,000 kroner, respectively.[108] In 1924/25, however, the good times were over. An annual income of 3,500 kroner was not much for five people to live on.[109]

When relatives invited Elias and Dora Lasnik to dinner, Dora Lasnik usually gave her daughters something to eat beforehand. That way they would not be ravenous when they arrived and their hosts would have no cause to think that the children got nothing to eat at home.[110] One time, however, Elise Lasnik wanted something good to eat and so she asked her mother to buy a little something on credit. Dora Lasnik answered: "The stomach doesn't have a window" and so it was rolled oats that day as well.[111] After all, no one could see what they had eaten, but if they bought something on credit, the entire town would become aware of it. Their mother used a pedal sewing machine to sew and repair their clothes. However, since her daughters did not have many clothes to their name, they sometimes had to stay home from school because their washed clothes had not dried during the night.[112]

Jenny Lasnik graduated from Møllergata School in June of 1921; she had completed five grades and was going to start middle school. Only 17 percent of the students in her class went on to middle school. The other students finished their last two years of elementary school.[113] Jenny Lasnik, however, began attending Borgerskolen, which was located near Wilses gate on the other side of Møllergata at Osterhausgaten 22. It was a public middle school that charged 300 kroner in annual fees. Nonetheless, along with seven of her eleven classmates, she received a scholarship and attended for free.[114] However, all students were responsible for buying their own books and writing materials.

In the spring of 1925, Jenny Lasnik passed her middle school exam with a grade of Satisfactory.[115] That fall she started on the two-year track at Oslo Commerce School. Her position at the school was only partially subsidized, and so she paid 150 kroner in school fees.[116] The two-year track included a theoretical and practical education in commerce, commercial law, economics, commercial arithmetic, bookkeeping, business correspondence and clerical work, product information that incorporated chemical and technical knowledge, geography, history, Norwegian, English, French, German, writing, touch typewriting, stenography (Gabelsberger's system) and Spanish. In the spring of 1927 she earned a grade of 2.11 on the final exam, which was one of the highest grades in her class. Of the 160 students on the two-year track in 1927, only nine were girls.[117]

Meanwhile, Anna Lasnik attended Møllergata School for seven years and finished in June of 1926. Her grades were high enough for her to have gone on to middle school, but she stayed home to help her mother with the house. Written Norwegian was her worst subject, as it was for her older sister.[118]

Elise Lasnik finished Møllergata School in the fifth grade and started middle school at Hammersborg School in August of 1925.[119] However, she did not have a free spot and so her school fees amounted to 8 kroner a month.[120] Taken together, the school fees for Jenny Lasnik and Elise Lasnik totaled 230 kroner in 1925/26. In addition to this sum, there were also books, paper, and writing materials to purchase. Elise Lasnik dreaded each time she had to ask her parents for money for an exercise book.[121]

As it turned out, Elise Lasnik was not accepted into the second year of middle school. Norwegian was also her worst subject and, apparently, it did not help that she was the best in her class at math. In the school records for class 1D, the column marked "promotion" is filled in with a "No."[122] She tried to continue at Vahl School, but they were not kind to Jews and so she quit.[123]

Elias and Dora Lasnik spoke Yiddish at home. When the children had friends over, they would whisper to their parents: "Speak Norwegian, speak Norwegian."[124]

6

Born Without Citizenship

On October 13, 1927, Dora Lasnik gave birth to another girl. A midwife assisted with the birth at Wilses gate 6.[125] Fourteen years had gone by since the last time that had happened. Jenny Lasnik, now eighteen, did not come home until late that evening; when she did, she acted as though nothing unusual had occurred. She thought her parents were too old for this nonsense; what could they want with another child? A couple of weeks passed before she actually paid the new family member much attention. Once that happened, however, the new little baby had to have the finest things they could possibly offer.[126] As long as Jenny Lasnik lived at home, she was the person to decide where the child went and what she did. When she moved out, Elise Lasnik took over responsibility for her little sister.

The older sisters would often dress up their little sister, put her in a stroller, and take her to Frogner Park or Ekebergsletta – that is, away from the noisy and polluted town center – so that she would get some fresh air.[127]

The month before the birth had been a difficult one. In August 1927, the family moved to an apartment on the fourth floor that had three rooms and a kitchen. Like their previous apartment, it was also located in stairway 1. The rent for this new apartment was 52 kroner a month, compared with the 38 kroner they had paid for the two-room apartment.[128] With a new child on the way, however, they needed the extra space. In addition, Jenny Lasnik was now able to contribute to the household income. She had taken her final exams at the business college and had secured her first office job. She now worked for Georg

Scheel,[129] a general manager at Claussen and Scheel A/S, whose firm, which specialized in bookbinder products, technical-chemical wares and plaster products, was located at Nedre Slotts gate 3.[130]

Even though nearly twenty years had passed since Elias and Dora Lasnik had first come to the city, the family was still stateless. Every change in address and work situation, not to mention new family additions, had to be recorded in Elias Lasnik's residency booklet. Accordingly, he visited the local police station in order to add Kathe Rita, as the child was to be called, to the booklet. The police also created a foreign registry card for her and put it into the index next to the others belonging to the Lasnik family. According to that card, "Kathe Rita," who "resided" in Oslo, was the "child of Elias Lasnik" and "without citizenship (Jew)."[131]

Just after her birth, Kathe Rita Lasnik was also registered in the Mosaic Religious Community. By 1927, this was the only Jewish religious community left in the city. The rest of the family had been members since January 1, 1921.[132] The Mosaic Religious Community was not large and Kathe Lasnik was the only newborn girl registered in 1927, though there had been five the previous year. Among them was Inger Becker, who would become friends with Kathe Lasnik. Celia Century was the first girl to be registered after Kathe Lasnik, and they would both attend the same class at Majorstua School.[133]

Both Inger Becker and Celia Century fled to Sweden in the fall of 1942. Although they both survived the war, neither of them lives in Norway. Celia Century resides in Jerusalem, while Inger Becker remained in Stockholm. I visited her there on April 25 and 26, 2001. The first day I was there, we sat at Cafe Milano on Kungsträdgården. We spent the next day at her house in Vestra Skogen, and she told me how Mr. Petersen, a teacher at Sinsen High School, had saved her family.

Celia Century occupied a small apartment in Jerusalem and I visited her there on March 24, 2001. She talked about how her family had fled to Sweden, about the awkward relationship that had developed between her and Kathe Lasnik when Kathe started attending

Majorstua School in January 1939, and about the poor quality of religious instruction they both had to endure at the Mosaic Religious Community.

After arriving in Sweden, Inger Becker and Celia Century both attended the Norwegian School. Inger Becker studied the English curriculum, Celia Century the math and science curriculum. In a book about the school published in 1975, 25 years after the school closed, Inger Becker appears in a class photograph (labeled 4 e.g.) taken in the fall of 1944, and Celia Century in a photograph (labeled 4 r.g.) taken in 1945.[134] Inger Becker also wrote one of the chapters in the book: "The School – As We Students Saw It Then."

By 1927, it had been many years since Elias Lasnik had found it necessary to fill out Oslo's annual census form himself. Instead, the elegant and clear handwriting that appears there belongs to his oldest daughters. The girls had also started helping him with invoices and bills.[135] On December 1, 1927, they had plenty of new information to add to the form: The family had moved to the fourth floor, Jenny Lasnik was an "office girl," Elias Lasnik had moved his workshop to Prinsens gate 12, and the family had a new member, Kathe Rita Lasnik.[136]

Directly to the right of the entryway in the new apartment was a door leading to the kitchen, which had a window overlooking the back yard. The kitchen was equipped with a gas jet for preparing food, a wood stove located just to the right of the door, cold running water and a sink. Another door led from the kitchen to a small room, which also had a window onto the backyard. The room behind the kitchen also had a door to the hallway, as well as a door to another room that had a window overlooking Wilses gate. The door to the left of the entryway led to the largest room in the apartment, which had two windows onto Wilses gate.

Today the apartment has been modernized. The front door opens right onto the kitchen; half of the small room behind the kitchen has been converted into a bathroom, while the kitchen has been widened to include both the other half of the room and the hallway, so that there are now two windows overlooking the backyard. The old oven is still there, but the wood stove just inside the kitchen door is gone. Marks on the polished wood floor, however, clearly show where it once stood. There are still black spots left by the fasteners that held the rectangular zinc or copper plate – upon which such stoves used to stand – away from the firewall. Indeed, with all the ash, wood, and splinters, the water that was toted to and from, and the stove rings that were put on or taken off, these wood stoves tended to make quite a mess. The debris escaped onto the floor, where staples and nails held the metal plate in place and left those black marks on the light wood, traces of the Lasnik family, not to mention the apartment's previous inhabitants.

The rooms were heated with wood, coal and coke; almost the whole cellar was taken up by fuel storage. Heating fouled the air, which eventually polluted the entire building. The cellar also had a laundry room and an ironing room.[137] The washtub was heated early in the morning; the clothes were boiled clean, rinsed, wrung out, and then carried up seven floors to the attic. The next day they were hauled down to the ironing room and pressed. There were women who went around the buildings and collected people's clothes. Whenever Dora Lasnik had the opportunity, she sent the wash out.[138] Every Sunday the Lasnik family went to the Torvgaten Bad,[139] where they could choose between a hot bath in a tub for 1.50 kroner, or a sauna or unmanned public bath with a shower for 0.75 kroner.[140]

Adolf Gorvitz, Elias Lasnik's tinsmith colleague, lived nearby with his wife and nine children in an apartment at Fredensborgveien 25. The apartment only had one room and a kitchen,[141] so there was barely enough floor space for them all to stretch out and sleep. Adolf Gorvitz kept a workshop at Ole Vigsgate 10, where his oldest son had worked since the year Kathe Lasnik was born, and where his second oldest, Moritz Gorvitz, would start as soon as he was finished with school. In the Gorvitz family, the parents also spoke Yiddish. The children understood what they were saying, but always answered in Norwegian.[142]

When Jenny Lasnik was born in 1909, her father was an apprentice tinsmith and her mother worked in a tobacco factory. Kathe Lasnik had a father who owned a tinsmith workshop and an older sister who was a qualified office assistant. The family belonged to another class in 1927, although the difference in their income was insignificant.

It was not only in the Lasnik family that children who lived at home contributed to the household income. Right across the corridor from the Lasniks lived Karl August Olsen from Borre, Norway, who was unemployed and had six children. His wife came from Larvik. All his children lived at home: Sigrid Olsen was 22 and a saleswoman on Bogstadsveien; Erling Olsen, who was 19, worked as a driver for Carl Hansen on Torvgaten; 17-year-old Ivar Olsen was an errand boy, while Randi Olsen at 15 was an errand girl; Reidar Olsen attended school; and the youngest child, who was six years old, stayed at home.[143] The third-floor apartment previously inhabited by the Lasniks was now let to two sisters: Dagmar Ruud, who was unmarried, and the widow Olga Olsen. Both were seamstresses. Olga Olsen's son was a sailor and his mother did not know his whereabouts. Therefore, she simply wrote, "sailor, address unknown" on the local municipal census form.[144]

When Kathe Lasnik was born, 81 people lived at Wilses gate 6: 31 had been born in Oslo; 38 had been born in Norway, though outside Oslo; 12 had been born in foreign countries, eight in Sweden and four in Russia. Besides the Lasniks, the other two from Russia were Markus Eliasson Levin, a retired religion instructor who was born in Vilna in 1855, and his wife, from Lettland.[145]

In the fiscal year of 1927/28, Elias Lasnik paid taxes on 4,000 kroner.[146] This sum included Jenny Lasnik's salary, which cannot have been much. Thanks to her education, however, she was employed during a year when 25 percent of union members in Oslo were unemployed. Although the family's income was not the absolute worst, only 1,000 out of Oslo's 110,000 taxpayers supported as many dependents on the same income as Elias Lasnik.[147] The following year he and his oldest daughter paid taxes on 5,500 kroner, and in 1928/29, when the crash of the New York stock market unleashed a worldwide economic depression, the Lasnik family's income stayed at 5,500 kroner.[148]

Not many people living at Wilses gate 6 were taxed on so high an income. In stairway 1, it was Gotfred Rönning, a commercial artist at Freia Chocolate Factory, who had the highest income at 6,400 kroner. Elias Lasnik, together with his oldest daughter, came in second.[149]

Wilses gate 4 has a reddish-yellow brick façade, while number 6's façade is covered with yellow stones. The borders around the windows, however, are exactly the same. Both buildings were designed by Eduard Carlén,[150] an architect known for his French Renaissance-inspired plastered brick structures.[151] The decoration adorning the space between each floor consists of a shield surrounded by oak leaves, and above every window on the fourth floor a man's head is staring down onto Wilses gate with a serious expression. Behind the building block, between the backyards and the rail fence that borders Christ Cemetery, a narrow footpath once ran between Møllergaten and Deichmans gate. The children used to call this path "Narrow Way." A deaf-mute shoemaker's shop was there, as well as Mrs. Nilsen's Milk Outlet.[152]

Wilses gate is just a little stump of a street running a few hundred meters between Møllergata and Fredensborgveien. A stone stairway divides it in two and helps ensure that it does not become steep.

The first floor of Wilses gate 6 now contained a notions shop and a grocery store. Lovise Othelie Eilertsen from Leirvik had moved into the Lasnik family's fruit store and ran Øijor, an ironing shop. The Mosaic Religious Community also had a meat market in the building.

The building's owner, Josef Koritzinsky, had in fact helped found the Mosaic Religious Community in 1892.[153] In 1927, however, there was a dispute over the meat market. Animal Protection, acting with Aker's chief of police, Johan Søhr, at its head, wanted to prohibit Jews from following their religious practices and engaging in what the police chief called a meaningless and gruesome "ritual slaughter."[154] A series of protests followed the proposal of the law, which would interfere with Jewish religious practices. Johan Søhr, for his part, claimed that he had recognized "one of the world's most wealthy Jewish moneymen and bankers" among the protesters. Jens Hunseid, the head of the Farmers' Party, was also unwilling to give the Jewish Religious Community any dispensation. As he put it: "We have no obligation to deliver our livestock up to the Jews' atrocities. We did not invite Jews to our country, and we have no obligation to provide the Jews with animals for their religious orgies."[155] In 1929, the law was accepted without dispensation, rendering a pointed observation that had been made by Carl Joachim Hambro, the Conservative Party's leading parliamentarian, even more relevant: "The practice of exaggerated animal protection usually happens at the expense of human victims."[156]

7

The Lasniks Become Norwegian Citizens

AT THE END of January, 1931, Elias Lasnik submitted an application for Norwegian citizenship to the Ministry of Justice. The application had also been written on behalf of his wife and two youngest daughters. In this document, Elias Lasnik explained that he had permanently resided in Oslo since he had arrived in the city in 1908, and, furthermore, that he had earned 3,500 kroner in 1929/30. The last question on the application read: "Reason I am seeking Norwegian citizenship." Elias Lasnik answered: "I plan on staying here in the future."[157]

Did this answer imply that from 1908 to 1930 Elias Lasnik had actually considered moving elsewhere? Probably not. Instead, the application for Norwegian citizenship would ideally be accompanied by an attest from the applicant's country of origin stating that the individual no longer had any obligations there. It was, however, impossible for Jewish emigrants from Vilna to procure such documentation. Czarist Russia no longer existed and Vilna had since been incorporated into Poland. There were some exceptions to this general rule: one was Isak Leimann, another was the tobacco factory owner Moritz Glott.[158] However, this is the actual reason that so many Russian Jews remained stateless or, like Elias Lasnik, only applied for Norwegian citizenship after they had already been in the country for decades. As a result, it was not by choice or politics that these individuals were drawn into Norwegian society, but rather by the residency booklet that obliged them to report to the police.

Since the application had also been submitted on Dora Lasnik's behalf, Elias Lasnik included a statement from her: "I [...] consent in my husband's application for Norwegian citizenship and desire that the authorization include me and my children under the age of 18."

All information given on the application had to be documented: for example, the fact that the applicant, Elias Lasnik, "speaks and writes Norwegian," that he had "conducted honorable business," and that he was "presumed able to provide for himself and his family." Manager Herman Bernstein, from Nordstrandshøgda, and his brother-in-law, Moritz Meieranovski, witnessed the documentation. The credibility of both men was further corroborated by the local police station.[159]

The Oslo tax collector also confirmed that Elias Lasnik had paid all his state taxes, the chief municipal treasurer that he had paid all city taxes. Oslo's Board of Guardians of the Poor affirmed that the applicant had never been on welfare, and so was presumed to be able to provide for himself and his family for as long as he was employed and employable.

In the investigative division at Oslo Police Headquarters, Reidar Sveen could not find that the "applicant" had ever been "indicted or punished for any offenses." Marius Holter, also of Oslo's investigative division, consulted the Registry of Aliens, which indeed showed that Elias Lasnik had resided in the city since he arrived in 1908, that he had not been "fined," had not appeared in any police reports and, indeed, had not had "anything to do with the police" in general. Constable Holter also took into consideration that the "applicant" owned his own tinsmith workshop, and had three adult daughters, two of whom held an "office job" in Oslo.

After the documents and attests had been reviewed, the Ministry of Justice's Police Office noted that the applicant was a Jewish tinsmith from Vilna, that he had come to Norway in 1908, that he was married to a "Polish-born [woman]," and had two children under 18. "Respectable," concluded the executive officer, who also noted that Elias Lasnik "considered himself to be stateless." The police could find no objections; the county recommended that the application be granted. Apparently, however, that was not enough. Before the executive officer actually reached a decision, he had to appeal to current practice, namely, that the Ministry had lately "been fairly reasonable with respect to granting Norwegian citizenship to Jews. The app[licant] has been in Norway for 22 years. I believe that the application could be granted." The executive officer drafted this resolution on a typewriter. Seeming to moderate himself somewhat, he went back, crossed out "could," and handwrote "ought to": "I believe that the application ought to be granted."[160]

A week later – that is, on March 30, 1931 – both the Justice and the Police Ministries had reached their decision. After Elias and Dora Lasnik had "pledged constitutional allegiance" in the presence of a judge, citizenship papers would be processed. Elias and Dora Lasnik, therefore, did just that in Oslo City Court on May 5; on May 26 their citizenship papers were issued. It was then noted on the cards in the foreign registry that Elias and Dora Lasnik, along with their two youngest daughters, had become Norwegian citizens.[161] "Norwegian citizenship"[162] was further stamped on their cards in the national registry.

Elias Lasnik could safely relinquish his residency booklet. From now on, it was only Jenny Lasnik and Anna Lasnik who were required to keep one. Their father had not included them on his citizenship application, undoubtedly because they were already guaranteed Norwegian citizenship by Section Two of the citizenship law: people who were born in Norway and had lived there "continuously for a full 22 years" were automatically granted Norwegian citizenship.[163] As a result, Jenny Lasnik became a Norwegian citizen in 1931, while Anna Lasnik had to wait until 1933.

The Central Bureau of Statistics painted the Norway of 1931 in dark terms. The economic crisis was larger than "any previous known crisis, and at year's end the international situation is as serious as it can possibly be."[164] Those words, however, were not applicable to the Lasnik family. After studying bookkeeping, stenography and typing, Elise Lasnik had found an office position at Standard Oil Company[165] in the winter of 1931. She earned 30 kroner a week.[166] Since 1929, Jenny Lasnik had worked at the Søndenfjeldske Steamboat Company at Prinsens gate 1. The first year she submitted a tax return was 1930/31, and her income was 2,000 kroner. That same year Elias Lasnik paid taxes on 4,000 kroner, a sum which included Elise Lasnik's salary. In one of the worst years of the economic crisis, then, the family had even managed to increase their income. Instead of two, they now had three family members working and collectively paid taxes on 6,500 kroner.[167]

8

Solid Laws and German Competence

WHEN KATHE LASNIK turned four in 1931, her sisters were already 22, 20, and 18 years old. She grew up surrounded by five adults. Might she have felt somewhat lonely?

Anna Lasnik had not merely helped her mother at home while Jenny Lasnik and Elise Lasnik worked as "office girls." She had also attended business school.[168] By the end of 1931, the sisters had saved enough money to open their own store. After looking around, they decided on a location in a building on the corner of Trondhjemsveien and Heimdalsgaten. They paid the first few months' rent in cash and they purchased their wares on credit from wholesalers.[169] It was easy to open a store, but difficult to make it profitable.

Trondhjemsveien Notions and Perfumery[170] opened its doors in 1931 under Jenny Lasnik's name.[171] Although she had the business license, she continued working at the Søndenfjeldske Steamboat Company. Instead, it was Anna Lasnik and Elise Lasnik who stood behind the counter.[172] Elise Lasnik welcomed the chance to quit Standard Oil Company, because the boss liked to touch the office girls.[173]

In January 1932, when registered unemployment among trade union members was 30 percent,[174] everyone in the Lasnik family had a job. Still, it was not a promising time to start a business; on top of that, there were already around 150 notions shops in the city.[175] It could not have been too bad, however, because Dora Lasnik was again able to hire domestic help in the form of 17 year-old Othelie Tønnesen from Mandal.[176]

On Wilses gate, everything was almost as it had been prior to 1933. The Olsen family still lived across the corridor from the Lasniks. The father was unemployed, but the wife had a washing job and all the children, with the exception of Reidar Olsen, also worked.[177] On the first floor, the Mosaic Religious Community's meat market had moved out, and Juridisk Forlag A/S – a legal publisher responsible for the distribution of the annual publication *Rettens gang* – had moved in. The ironing shop, Øijor, was still there and Miss Lovise Othelie Eilertsen still lived in the back room.[178]

Outside of Wilses gate, however, significant changes were taking place. Immediately after Adolf Hitler was named chancellor of Germany in January 1933, the Norwegian ambassador in Berlin was asked if German Jews could get permission to come to Norway. The ambassador asked the Foreign Ministry for "guidelines."[179] The letter was sent from the Foreign Ministry to the Ministry of Justice, and was forwarded to the Central Passport Office. This office answered that German Jews should appeal to the legation in Berlin and should include information on their background, education, and personal assets. The Ministry of Justice added that each application would be considered on an individual basis. Finally, before the answer was sent back to the Berlin legation, the Foreign Ministry had its say: "The high unemployment rate and depressing economic conditions unfortunately make it difficult to provide a place for Germans seeking to leave Germany because of the present situation."[180] The Foreign Ministry also added a handwritten note regarding the communiqué from the Ministry of Justice. "A reasonable remark! For once, just as reasonable as that of the Central Passport Office! [...] this ques. is so large that it does not hurt to view it from a more general perspective. An invasion of Jews is, namely, something we want to avoid. (Even though in our hearts we feel all possible sympathy with them.)"[181]

When National Socialist Germany arranged an official boycott of all Jewish businesses at the beginning of April 1933, *Aftenposten* discussed the event in the editorial section. The political editor Johaness Nesse was worried, because "Germany's recent campaign against the

Jews stirs up Jewish sympathy across the globe, which these sons of Israel hardly deserve." In Norway itself there were no "grounds to form a just opinion regarding the anti-Jewish campaigns. We do not know to what extent the German people's suffering can be blamed on Jewish methods and mentality. We only know that these are now despised, and we can conclude from this that [the campaign] is not due to feelings of inferiority and envy, but has actual causes." The newspaper, however, was also worried about Germany, because "Jewish retaliation" from abroad would certainly strike the Germans, who were isolated, "a race confined behind walls," and retaliation could hinder the reconstruction of Germany: "We can only express our regret should the work of rebuilding be hindered by a too hasty and violent confrontation with the Jews." All the contributions *Aftenposten* had been receiving regarding the persecution of Jews in Germany during the spring of 1933 further convinced Nesse that "here in this country" there was also "considerable anti-Semitism." According to the editor, the Jews had "a special ability and a particular talent of seeing possibilities in and ways out of every situation," which must be met "with solid laws, with German competence and with stronger supervision."[182]

In 1933, Elias Lasnik also moved his workshop with all its equipment from Storgaten 26 to Brogaten 6.[183] The new workshop was located in a one-story annex in the back yard. (In Storgaten, it had been located in a cellar within the building itself.)[184] During that first year, his income was low. He only paid taxes on 3,000 kroner. Jenny Lasnik, who paid taxes on 1,700 kroner, also earned less than the year before. In addition, the two sisters running the shop, which they now called Trondhjemsveien Perfumery,[185] were not taxed at all, so they could not have had much of a salary.[186] Even though five people in the family were now working, compared with three earlier, the household income shrank to 4,700 kroner.

During the summer of 1933, Jenny Lasnik was given a free trip to France on one of the boats belonging to the Søndenfjeldske Steamboat Company. She traveled to Paris, bringing with her the address of a Norwegian man, Leopold Bermann, who was studying medicine at the Sorbonne. Leopold had been born in Latskova in Russia in 1903. His father, a merchant, had brought his family to Norway in 1906. Eventually, the 24-year-old office assistant, Jenny Lasnik, and the 30-year-old medical student, Leopold Bermann, became a couple.[187]

In December of 1933, it was Anne Marie Kolloen from Nord-Fron in Gudbrandsdalen who, for a krone a day plus room and board,[188] helped Dora Lasnik around the house.[189] Born in 1909, she was, I found, still listed in the telephone book. When I called, she answered, but could not understand what I said. So I wrote her a letter, included a copy of the census record from 1933, and asked if she was the Anne Marie Kolloen who had provided domestic help for the Lasnik family in January, 1933. A few days after I had sent the letter, I called her. Yes, it was her, but she could not remember much; she thought she had only been there a couple of weeks before getting sick. In the Lasnik apartment, the maid lived in a small enclosure separated by a curtain in the small entryway; she had lain there, unable to move. She remembered that every room had beds, which were leaned up against the wall during the day. The maid from Nord-Fron immediately perceived that she had gotten a job in a poor household; after all, they had next to nothing. Still, they had been kind to her. She also remembered that they ran a store, but that was all.[190]

9

Kathe Lasnik Starts School

KATHE LASNIK REGISTERED for class 1A at Møllergata School in August, 1934. Her teacher was 42-year-old Jenny Wiborg. Miss Wiborg had been at the elementary school since 1915 and had received all five age-determined pay increments of 375 kroner each, so that her yearly salary totaled 5,400 kroner. Male teachers with the same level of seniority earned 7,000 kroner a year.[191]

The architect Jacob Nordan had designed all the buildings at Møllergata School, which dated from 1861, in an early Florentine Renaissance style.[192] The school had 33 classrooms, two workshops, natural science and crafts rooms, two choir rooms, an art room, a school kitchen, a clinic, a dental office with two rooms, two rooms for the male and female teachers, two equipment rooms and a cafeteria.

The new gym was finished in 1933. It could be divided into two parts, and each half came equipped with a changing room and a shower.[193] The old outhouses had been replaced by bathrooms, and the classroom furnaces by a coal-fired central heating system.[194]

The principal's residence, furthermore, had a kitchen, a bath and seven rooms,[195] showing that being the principal of an elementary school in the capital city was an important position.

When Kathe Lasnik started first grade, the school had 1,029 students. There were 61 boys and 71 girls in the first grade, which had been separated into two all-boys and three all-girls classes. After a short time, however, the three all-girls classes were reduced to two, which meant that class 1A ended up with 30 students.[196]

The girls' building faced Møllergata, while the boys' building faced Deichmans gate. The principal's residence and the gym were located right in the middle of the yellow line that divided the schoolyard into girls' and boys' areas.

Indeed, the one thing that broke the severe symmetry was a brand new building with a swimming pool that faced Deichmans gate. The pool measured 12.5 x 8 meters and the building would eventually have a new cafeteria on the top floor.[197] However, the construction was not yet finished in the fall of 1934.

In terms of the breadwinners who provided for the girls in class 1A, 12 were manual laborers, three were tradesmen, three were master tradesmen, three were functionaries, two were merchants, and the remainder included a policeman, a second lieutenant, a radio operator, a chemical engineer, a janitor and a sculptor.[198]

The rules laid down by Oslo's School Board regarding absences were pasted into Miss Jenny Wiborg's school journal for class 1A. "Prestedage," days devoted to church activities, were registered with a "p" and "Jews' and Adventists' absence due to a holy day" were marked with an "h," but were not counted as an absence. Kathe Lasnik was excused from classes in religious instruction, and therefore did not have to participate in activities related to Christianity. However, she did attend school on Saturdays and read, wrote and drew, which Orthodox Jews were supposed to refrain from doing.[199]

During the first half-year, Kathe Lasnik had only one absence – September 19 – and that absence was excused. On November 28, however, she was tardy.[200] Miss Jenny Wiborg never marked Kathe Lasnik's absences as unexcused. She always used a "t" for an absence with permission or "tillatelse," or an "s" if the absence was due to sickness.

The same year that Kathe Lasnik started school, her older sister, Jenny Lasnik, quit her job at the Søndenfjeldske Steamship Company and began working at A/S Stormbull, Oslo's largest iron wholesaler. Together, Kathe's father and three older sisters paid taxes on 9,200 kroner in 1934/35.[201] Anna Lasnik and Elise Lasnik had also opened a new shop at Markveien 58, which is located right next to the Anker

Bridge in lower Grünerløkka, in 1934. The new shop was called Markveien Kitchen Supplies, and Elise Lasnik ran it during the first year. The next year, however, they traded places: Anna Lasnik stayed at Markveien, while Elise Lasnik ran Trondhjemsveien Kitchen Supplies.[202]

The poor economic conditions led to increased competition. An editorial addressing this fact appeared in the trade periodical of the Tinsmith Masters' League. The editorial, entitled "Trade Parasites – Outsiders," argued that "any and all means necessary should be permitted"[203] in the fight against those operating outside the organization. The name Hermann Gettler appeared often. When I visited Moritz Gorvitz again, he affirmed that Hermann Gettler was indeed the third Eastern European Jewish tinsmith in Oslo. Since the municipal census forms are organized by address, I had to know where Gettler had lived in order to find his form. For this reason, I consulted the Oslo Address Book from 1935, which then enabled the City Archives to find the form. I learned that Hermann Gettler originated from Libau, and that he kept a workshop at Ruseløkkbasaren 57. He had worked there together with his two sons, although he also had three daughters who worked in a shop and at a factory. The whole family had lived in a two-room apartment located in a shabby back building at Akersveien 21.[204]

The three Jewish tinsmiths were not the only ones accused of unlawful trade practices, but they were the ones who were often named in the masters' periodical. In the spring of 1934, it was Elias Lasnik's turn to be fined 50 kroner. However, he had just paid a fine of 25 kroner, and so he refused to pay the new penalty.

The matter made its way to Oslo City Court and a hearing was held on September 14, 1934. Unlawful activity was said to have taken place when Elias Lasnik repaired the gutters on Oscarsgate 67. After the court had considered the conflicting accounts, it decided that Elias Lasnik indeed "owed the fine" and that a fitting punishment would be a 50 kroner penalty payable to the public treasury. Taking a stricter approach, the court emphasized the fact that Elias Lasnik had already been fined 25 kroner for unlawful activity; from a more lenient perspective, however, it also emphasized the "economic situation of the accused."[205]

In April, 1935, Elias Lasnik was again cited for operating "with paid outside help" and was fined 100 kroner. Again, he refused to pay the sum and, just as before, the matter was sent to Oslo City Court, which heard the case on September 9, 1935.

Elias Lasnik explained that Kristian Sæter had indeed helped with a job on the Telegraph Building at Prinsensgate 20, but that the work was "handyman labor in keeping with what is allowed by Section 13 of the trade law." Kristian Sæter, that is, had simply set up and screwed in "ready-made gutter pipes where corresponding pipes had been previously located." "In the opinion of the accused," the task was not "craftmanswork, but rather handyman work."

Nonetheless, the court found that Elias Lasnik had to be "found guilty." However, it also took into account that "for the accused, the present case partly revolves around a matter of principle." Therefore, in the opinion of the court, "the accused [should not] be sentenced to pay a penalty of more than 50 kroner." From a stricter perspective, the court noted that he had already been fined twice before; from a more lenient perspective, the "economic situation of the accused"[206] was again taken into account.

10

A Little Israelite

WHEN HER DAUGHTERS worked long hours at their shops, Dora Lasnik would sometimes bring them lunch. One time, however, Elise Lasnik brought an employee home for lunch. When they got back to the shop, the employee said something like: "My goodness, it's so clean there" or "Your house really was clean."[207] In other words, she was surprised to find that a Jewish family kept their house clean.

The annual census form was due in December 1935. On it residents were required to state if they had been unemployed; lost workdays due to "sickness, strike or lockout" did not count. Elias Lasnik calculated half a year of unemployment, Jenny Lasnik 38 days. Of course, they were not the only ones to record similar information. In Wilses gate 6, there were 10 other people without work.[208] It was not simply unemployment, however, that worried the Lasnik family. During the night, they were often awakened by Elias Lasnik's cough.[209]

Still, in December 1935, Leopold Bermann, then a medical student, came to visit his girlfriend, Jenny Lasnik. The municipal census form records that he was set to arrive from Paris on December 4 and that he occupied the civil status of "future son-in-law."[210] Things lightened up with the visit from Paris. Though Leopold Bermann's parents lived in the city of Trondhjem, he planned to spend his vacation with his future in-laws. Dora Lasnik spoiled him thoroughly.[211]

At this time, Kathe Lasnik, now in class 2A, had free meals at school.[212] She was one of the 19,000 students in the Oslo school system who received one free meal a day during the 1935/36 school year if they wanted it or if the school decided that they needed it.

At Majorstua and Bolteløkka schools, five percent of the students received a free meal, though at Møllergata that number rose to 20 percent. In Miss Jenny Wiborg's class, 14 of the 30 students arrived for their free breakfast at 8:00 a.m. Supervisory teacher Gunvor Eg went to get the children. While the children marched up the stairs to the cafeteria on the fourth floor, however, she took the elevator. The cafeteria had 18 long tables, all set with heavy plates containing two pieces of bread and a small bowl of milk. On the inside of the bowl was the Oslo city coat of arms with the motto *unanimiter et constanter*, united and steadfast. Painted on the white end wall in the cafeteria was the motto: "Do not drink with food in your mouth full."[213]

The girls in class 2A thought it was exciting to have Kathe Lasnik in class. They had learned that Jews were God's chosen people. One time, when Miss Jenny Wiborg wanted to emphasize a story, she went up to Kathe Lasnik, laid a hand on her dark hair, and turned to the class: "And here you see a little Israelite."[214] This is the one single statement from a teacher to or about Kathe Lasnik that has survived in memory to this day.

Another time, the class was talking about the royal family. Eva Thornæs had said something or other about Queen Maud, and suddenly Kathe Lasnik laughed: "She said Måd, but her name is Maud."[215] Eva Thornæs, however, had pronounced the queen's name correctly. Her father was a master tinsmith and had told her that things were not going all that well for Kathe Lasnik's father.

In 1934, the Labor Party won the municipal election in Oslo for the third time. As a result Jørgen Borgen from the Labor Party became chair of the municipal education board. Energetically following in the tracks of his political predecessors, he saw to it that a number of measures were set in place: sexual education was introduced, the number of students per class was reduced, an educational research institute was established, and courses were organized for unemployed youth. The municipal school board also raised the number of study hours for first grade from 18 to 24 hours a week.[216]

Furthermore, swim meets, ski jumping and downhill races would be held to help foster hygiene, health, physical control and competition. In addition, the school doctor strongly advocated weekly baths instead of one every other week. Showering after gym was also important, both "in terms of cleanliness and in the building of resilience." Indeed, the school doctor condemned "a bad habit" that seemed to be spreading, namely, that students were using "gym clothes as their underclothes in the morning" and then were keeping them on all day.[217]

The Oslo schools also pioneered the use of film in education. The films *Hungary, Holland* and *Lancashire at Work* were among those shown to almost all public school students during the 1935/36 school year. Through the schools' "film circulation," movies such as *Fredrikstad, Nes Ironworks, Norway's Grain Supply* I, II, and III and *Spring in Hardanger* became welcome aids in geography instruction, while science classes made good use of *The Beaver, The Hedgehog, The Chicken, Gulls and Terns*.[218]

When Prime Minister Mowinckel left office in 1935, there was little doubt that Johan Nygaardsvold and the Labor Party would form a government. The non-socialist parties indeed gave in, and from day one Johan Nygaardsvold and the Labor Party put forward a resolute program to battle the economic crisis and unemployment.

Eva Petersen, the daughter of the janitor at People's House, was in Kathe Lasnik's class. It was her father who raised the red flags for the observance of Labor Day at Youngstorvet on May 1 every year. Aslaug Ligård, another girl from the class, lived at Wilses gate 2 and wanted to watch the flag raising, but could not get permission. A few people hung out their laundry in protest, while others stuck small flags out of the window. Karen Swärd, another student in 2A, lived next to the Eldorado Movie Theater at Torvgaten 11; every year she and her parents participated in the May 1 celebration. During that entire afternoon workers from Grünerløkka dressed in suits would stream up Brenneriveien and through Møllergaten to join the parade.[219]

There were huge May 1 demonstrations in both 1935 and 1936. In 1936 the festivities began at 8:30 a.m. with a flag parade in front of the People's House and a song performed by the Oslo Workers' Choir Association. After that, the main demonstration proceeded from Youngstorvet to Festningsplassen. There were slogans like "Today 2/3 of Norwegian people earn below 2,000 kroner a year" and "People's wages and living standards must be improved." International slogans, however, also made an appearance. "Fight for Ernst Thälemann's freedom," a slogan supporting the German Communist Party leader, imprisoned since Adolf Hitler came to power, could be seen, as well as "Unity against war and fascism."[220]

At Festningsplassen the Minister of Justice, Trygve Lie, gave the keynote speech. The next day Arbeiderbladet, a labor newspaper, reported on the "auspicious May 1 under brilliant sun."[221] Norway, in fact, had not seen a larger political gathering since the cost-of-living demonstrations during World War I. Even though the demonstration's main slogans – "We're rallying for a labor victory in the parliamentary election of 1936" and "This year we'll have the majority" – failed to materialize, Johan Nygaardsvold's government remained in place.

It was some time, however, before the initiatives against unemployment implemented by the new Labor Party-led government took effect. It did not help matters that those born during the baby boom of the 1920s began to enter the work force in the mid-1930s, making it even more difficult to bring down unemployment. 1935 and 1936 were the worst years of all, and for some of the students at Møllergata School the milk, bread with cod-liver spread and cheese, along with a carrot or an apple afterwards, was the only real meal they got during the day. There were rumors of children given a nip at bedtime so that hunger would not plague them at night. One of the girls in 2A, who lived in a hovel in Hammersborg, showed up one day carrying her schoolbooks in a paper bag. Her backpack had been pawned.[222]

11

Bridesmaid

THE LASNIK FAMILY only paid taxes on 6,600 kroner in 1935/36.[223] Elias Lasnik himself had earned next to nothing. Nonetheless, after 24 years at Wilses gate 6, the family moved to an apartment with four rooms, a maid's room, and a kitchen at Fredensborgveien 2. The rent was 140 kroner a month. By the time the family moved in on April 1936,[224] Kathe Lasnik had almost finished second grade. However, moving did not mean that she would change schools. The new apartment was only 300-400 meters away from Møllergata School, just behind Deichmanske Library and Trinity Church.

The building at Fredensborgveien 2 was built in the 1870s and had two apartments on each of its three floors. The Lasnik apartment on the third floor had running water, cooking gas, and electricity, although the toilet was located in the back yard. Once again, the family needed more space; by this time, Leopold Bermann had joined them. He was no longer a student, but held a medical degree from Paris. Since he had taken his medical exams in a foreign country, however, he had to seek permission to practice medicine in Norway. When he was denied it, he took the dental exam and was immediately hired by Lier Asylum.

In the meantime, 41-year-old Alvide Rønning from Nes in Romerike occupied the maid's room and provided domestic help, while another room was let out to 29-year-old Julie Hansen, who served coffee at Carlos Restaurant.[225]

Though the occupants of the other apartments in the building belonged, like the Lasniks, to the lower middle class and liberal professions, they had to supplement their income by renting out rooms in the large and expensive apartments. In fact, the practice was so widespread that the building gave the impression of being a collection of studio apartments for workers.

In 1936, Møllergata School could finally put to use what the head of school health services in Oslo, Dr. L. Stoltenberg, characterized as "the big, beautiful and hygienically built swimming pool."[226] Access to a swimming pool was especially important for students living in the city center or on the east side who had no baths at home. Therefore, Møllergata and Sagene were the first schools in Oslo to get swimming halls. The students had no idea that while they were busy swimming, Gunvor Eg was in the changing room checking whether their underclothes were neat and clean.[227]

During the 1936/37 school year, the city of Oslo spent 321.52 kroner per student, 4 kroner more than the year before.[228] However, there were quite a few things that the municipal education board thought still needed to be fixed. In some schools, students had to wear coats in the classrooms; other schools had such poor ventilation systems that the air quality seemed "unhealthy for teachers' and students' well-being." Yet another problem was that many of the students used desks that were two or three sizes too small.

It was uncommon for the girls in Miss Jenny Wiborg's class to hold a birthday party, but Karin Swärd was an only child and did just that. Her mother insisted that Kathe Lasnik be invited, since it was her understanding that Kathe Lasnik was not included all that often. For some people, of course, a birthday invitation could present a problem, because it required them to buy a gift. Nonetheless, Kathe Lasnik went to Karin Swärd's party. Her friend's father was a plumber and was active in the union. Her mother was also a member of the workers' movement and thought that a person's religion or their parents' country of origin should make no difference in how they were treated.[229]

Nonetheless, there were not many adults who understood that simply failing to exclude someone was not enough. Instead, it was necessary to make an active effort to include them. A couple of years later, art historian Nic. Stang invited tobacco factory owner Moritz Glott to his house for the evening – among other things, because Glott had donated money to help German refugees gain asylum in Norway. During the evening, Glott, who occupied the social position of a well-to-do factory owner, told Stang that despite the many years he had lived in Norway, this was the first time that he had been invited into a Norwegian home.[230]

Kathe Lasnik and Karin Swärd also spent time together after school. They went down Hausmanns gate and over Anker Bridge, with its sculptures by Dyre Vaa, to the stores on Markveien. Anna Lasnik would let them come in and look at the small knick-knacks and other things for sale in a kitchen supply shop. Sometimes, though, they also went to Kathe Lasnik's house. Her mother always gave them a warm welcome. It was obvious that Dora Lasnik was pleased that her daughter had brought a friend home, and she made an effort to be accommodating and to make things as comfortable for them as possible.[231]

When the rest of the class had Christian religious instruction, however, Kathe Lasnik left the room. Karin Swärd was always curious about where Kathe Lasnik went and what she did at these times. Did she stand out in the hallway or pace back and forth in the schoolyard? She wanted badly to ask, but never worked up the courage.[232]

Public school students were entitled to a single field trip during the interwar period, and so Miss Jenny Wiborg took her class on a day trip to the famous sluice gates at Haldens and Tistedals Waterways. Huge steamships went right up to Tistedals Waterfall. At the top of the falls, smaller ships carried passengers and cargo to the towns located in the deep woods between Norway and Sweden. Karin Johanne Skoglund, née Swärd, thought that she remembered that Kathe Lasnik had been on the field trip to Halden. There had been quite a commotion on the train, because the boys' class was also making a trip to the waterways. The teacher had had quite a time trying to keep the classes separated, and finally she had asked the conductor to close the door to the car where the boys were sitting.

Did Kathe Lasnik actually go on that field trip? She stopped attending Møllergata School in July 1938 and the field trip took place that summer. It could have been before they finished fourth grade in June 1938, or after they started fifth grade in August, or perhaps even at the beginning of September. None of the girls with whom I had spoken earlier had mentioned the field trip and it was not possible to find an answer to the question.

While I was visiting Aslaug Ligård, she asked Synnøve Agdestein, now Vinje, who had also been in the class, to come over. I had brought with me a copy of the class ledger, and we talked about each girl: where she had lived, what her father's job had been and with whom she had been friends.

Aslaug Ligård, who had lived on the same block as Kathe Lasnik, told me about the gangs of boys who would come up Brenneribakken from Grünerløkka. The people on Wilses gate considered the people living on the other side of the Aker River to be at least one social class below them. The rabble from Vaterland who wandered the area every now and then lacked social status entirely.

Aslaug Ligård and Synnøve Vinje thought that Kathe Lasnik might have sat next to Edith Halvorsen from Øvre gate or Gerd Hansen from Wessels gate. She had sat at the front of the room in the row next to the wall. However, Edith Halvorsen, now Harboe, could not remember ever having sat next to Kathe Lasnik. The Kongsvinger Special Registry, furthermore, was not able to find Gerd Hansen. I did manage to find Liv Larsen, who had lived with her mother at Rostedsgate 1 in 1938. She had sat next to Kathe Lasnik; they had been best friends, she said, and she had been to Kathe Lasnik's house many times.

When Jenny Wiborg's class held a reunion 50 years after taking their elementary school exams, Aslaug Ligård read aloud the description of the area around Møllergata School from Olav Angell's book *Oslo in Twilight*. She recalled the delicatessen that had been at Møllergaten 46 or 48 and the wonderful smell of fish cakes and fish pudding that came wafting out of it. Aslaug Ligård and Synnøve Agdestein were not sure if Kathe Lasnik had attended school on Saturdays, but they thought she probably had, given that Jenny Wiborg's school journal had marks for every day and every student, including Kathe Lasnik on Saturdays. Synnøve Vinje also remembered that Kathe Lasnik ate fish pudding every Saturday. That was how she had celebrated the Jewish Sabbath.

The girls from the class played together in the schoolyard, and their most adventurous game involved pushing each other over the yellow line separating the girls' and boys' sides. When they played hide-and-seek in Wilses gate after school, however, Kathe Lasnik was not often with them. As a rule, she went straight home.[233]

Nonetheless, during the winter she went ice-skating with Aslaug Ligård and Grace Qvarnström, who was also from the class. They were too young to go to Bislett Sports Stadium, where there was music. The nearest skating rink was at Falck Ytters Square between Bjerregaards gate and Waldemar Thranes gate. Every now and then, though, they went to the skating rink at Alexander Kiellands Square a little farther away.[234]

Though Elias Lasnik still kept a workshop at Brogaten 6, he did not pay taxes on more than 1,100 kroner in 1936/37. His daughters paid taxes on 5,900 kroner.[235] Elias Lasnik coughed regularly now and the slightest effort got him out of breath. At the beginning of December 1936, he was admitted to Ullevål Hospital.[236] He was released on December 14, but on January 12, 1937, he was readmitted. From now on, it was the hard-working and considerate daughters who took care of their parents and Kathe Lasnik.

Leopold Bermann and Jenny Lasnik were married on November 7, 1937. Kathe Lasnik, who was a bridesmaid, wore a white dress and a headband decorated with cloth flowers. The day after the wedding, she missed school. Kathe Lasnik had not only been tardy on September 29, but also on October 6, 8, 15, 20, 26, 27, and 28. And on October 16 she was sick.[237] Why now? Earlier this had almost never happened. Did the wedding preparations cause her to oversleep? Was she afraid that she would miss her big sister or worried about what would happen after they moved out? Or was it her father's coughing that alarmed her at night? Did something unpleasant happen at school that made her want to avoid attending classes? No one could provide any answers to these questions.

Jenny Lasnik had had a boyfriend in Paris for a number of years. No doubt she had written him plenty of letters and had told him funny anecdotes about her little sister. These letters no longer exist. Jenny Bermann's daughter told me that Dora Lasnik had renewed contact with her mother and other relatives in the USA. She also mentioned that Kathe Lasnik was perhaps on a home movie that a relative from the USA had shot when he visited the Lasnik family in Oslo before the war. It is easy to imagine such a movie! However, it never turned up.

For a short time after they were married, Leopold and Jenny Bermann remained at Fredensborgveien 2. In the meantime, she quit Stormbull to work as a stenographer,[238] while he looked after the dental practice he had opened at Storgaten 37. In the beginning of 1938, however, the newly married couple moved to Ullevål Hageby in Vestre Aker. At this point, the maid was let go and the maid's room rented out to Judith Nelson, who worked at Astoria Hotel. With his chronic lung disease, tinsmithing work proved difficult for Elias Lasnik. In order to bring in a little money, he took a job at a restaurant laundry service[239] run by Paul Steffens and located at Chr. Krohgs gate 30.[240]

12

Will You Play With Me?

ON DECEMBER 21, 1938, when she was halfway through fifth grade, Kathe Lasnik, now eleven years old, left Møllergata School. The week before Christmas break, the Lasnik family relocated to Hertzbergs gate up in Fagerborg,[241] which was about as far west as you could go at the time and still remain in Oslo. The elegant Jacob Aalls gate was all that lay between Hertzbergs gate and Kirkeveien, which bordered what was then Aker municipality, later part of Oslo. Leopold and Jenny Bermann, who had become parents to a son in August, lived nearby in Ullevål Hageby.

Up to then, Elias and Dora Lasnik had only moved a couple of blocks or floors; this time they made quite a leap. Anna Lasnik and Elise Lasnik had found the family an apartment. Though Elias Lasnik no longer worked at the laundry service, he did as much as he could at his workshop on Brogaten. The year the family moved to Fagerborg, he paid taxes on 1,800 kroner,[242] about the same amount he had earned as an apprentice when he came to the city thirty years earlier. Sales in the two kitchen supply stores were well under 100 kroner a day and were a little higher in Markveien than in Trondhjemsveien. In 1937, sales at Markveien Kitchen Supplies amounted to 24,000 kroner, a gross profit of 5,700 kroner. The net profit, however, was barely 1,000 kroner.[243]

The Lasnik family apartment at Hertzbergs gate 7 had a bond of 3,500 kroner, though the rent was still 152.50 kroner a month. That was a lot for an apartment in Fagerborg Parish.[244] At the same time, the apartment into which they moved was also brand new, modern and in tiptop shape.

The five-floor apartment building, which was designed by Henrik Nissen and Gunnar Brynning,[245] was an isolated, functionalist-style rectangle surrounded by green spaces on all sides. Arriving at Hertzbergs gate from the center of the city was like coming to the country. Hertzbergs gate, furthermore, was a little stub of a street between Suhms gate and Jacob Aalls gate; with only eight addresses to its name, it was high above both the city center and Majorstua. The building had been erected on the site of the Prestenes Church rectory. Deciduous trees ringed the red brick building.

Hot water and central heating were included in the rent. The apartment had a bathroom with a toilet and a bathtub. The family even bought a new electric stove with the brand name "Lyn" ("Lightning").[246] They did not need to buy a refrigerator, however, since one was built into the kitchen. There was a fireplace in the living room, so the residents could warm themselves around a crackling fire on cold fall days. The Lasnik family also kept a copper pot next to the fireplace for firewood.[247] The apartment measured about 80 square meters and had two bedrooms and a large entry hall. The living room had a door onto a balcony facing Hertzbergs gate.

Across the street was Jessenløkken Housing Cooperative, with its 37 large apartment buildings. Each building had a gray-washed tile façade and contained three-, four- or five-room apartments. On the other side of the building, toward Stensparken, were residential streets full of yards with huge trees.

The new rectory with its eight rooms, hall, entryway and kitchen was located off staircase B. However, it also exited onto staircase A. Johan C. H. S. Prytz lived there with his wife and four children. Directly beneath the minister lived the building's modern couple: a man and woman who had no children and an extensive education. Apart from Prytz, it was only a machinist, a common worker, and tinsmith Elias Lasnik who could boast five to six people in their apartment.[248]

In January 1939 Kathe Lasnik started at Majorstua School in class 5C. The homeroom teacher was Rønnaug Heyerdahl Larsen. She had been with the school since its founding in 1908.[249] Like Møllergata School, Majorstua kept the boys and girls strictly separate. There were 27 girls in the new class, which in itself was a bit unusual. About half of the students, namely, had started school a year early. It was an experimental project, and the class had a reputation for being rambunctious.

The parents of the girls in 5C belonged to the upper mercantile class. Interestingly enough, there is no registered tinsmith among them; instead, Elias Lasnik called himself a "merchant."[250] In a way this was true. Elise Lasnik had helped her father to sell the largest pieces of his tinsmithing machinery. However, he still maintained a small workshop in Hausmanns gate.[251] For the most part, though, Elias Lasnik helped his daughters in their stores; however, his help was not always advantageous. Elias Lasnik was far too polite to the salesmen who came to the stores. He thought he had to buy a little of whatever they were selling, so at least they would be able to eat that day.[252]

Some consideration was given at Majorstua as to which of the girls' classes Kathe Lasnik should be placed in. The principal ultimately decided on 5C for a very specific reason[253] – namely, there was already one Jewish girl in the class, Celia Century. She was the daughter of David Century, a businessman who had emigrated from Poland to England in 1905 and to Norway in 1916. Her father, who had attended prestigious schools in England and had even studied medicine for a while, was an intellectual who educated his children in Jewish faith and history.[254]

The principal thought things would be easier for both Celia Century and Kathe Lasnik, since now there were two Jewish girls in the class. This was wrong: it made things worse for both of them. Because Celia Century grew up in an Orthodox family that took religion very seriously, she could neither write nor draw at school on Saturdays. Kathe Lasnik, on the other hand, both wrote and drew and she also wanted to learn about Christianity, even though she was exempted from the subject. This meant that the teachers and students could now look at Celia Century and think: Why does she make such a fuss about things? Kathe Lasnik is also Jewish, but on Saturday she reads and writes. Therefore, things definitely got worse for Celia Century when Kathe Lasnik joined the class. The others began to regard her as difficult. Celia Century, for her part, thought it was bad form for Kathe Lasnik to act as if she were not Jewish, but just like everyone else.[255]

However, it was also hard for Kathe Lasnik. Compared with Celia Century, who had a well-read father and was proud of her background and even emphasized it, Kathe Lasnik was not quite as quick-witted. Her parents only spoke broken Norwegian. Indeed, none of the people I interviewed could ever remember hearing Dora Lasnik say a word. Perhaps she did not want to embarrass her daughter.

Kathe Lasnik was not able to defend herself against Celia Century's accusation that she wanted to be like everyone else and so acted non-Jewish. One time, when she was about to break down in the schoolyard, Jannicke Didrichsen from the class intervened and stopped Celia Century.[256]

What was the difference between Kathe Lasnik and Celia Century? They stood out because they were Jewish, but there is always social pressure on those who depart from the norm. Kathe Lasnik gave into this pressure and wanted to be like everyone else; Celia Century insisted on being accepted despite her differences.

One afternoon, sometime in the winter of 1939, Kathe Lasnik went out to sled with Fride and Ingrid Prytz, the daughters of the fourth-floor minister. Suddenly, Kathe Lasnik stopped and asked: "Will you play with me?"[257] The question surprised the sisters, since they played with everybody. However, they realized that the girl from the first floor was not used to taking this for granted.

13

Corpses from *Blücher*

ONE DAY, WHILE sitting in the Oslo City Archives to find out exactly when Kathe Lasnik had registered at Majorstua School, I saw something unexpected. Right under her name on the registration list were eight other Jewish or maybe German names: Fritz Schreier, Edith Griser, Olga Feldtmann, Will Flechner, Robert Korn, Sigmund Korn, Alfred Fink and Josef Fenster. All had the same address: the Jewish Orphanage, Industrigaten 34. They had all come from Vienna.[258] The youngest was starting first grade, the oldest fourth grade. Why had no one in Kathe Lasnik's class mentioned them? Although I had talked to most of them a number of times, no one had said a word about these students. When all those Jewish students started school, had there not been some discussion as to why they were there? On top of this, they started only a few months after Kathe Lasnik transferred from Møllergata School.

As it turns out, a committee had made it possible for twenty poor Jewish children from Vienna to spend their summer vacation in Norway in 1938. The children arrived in Oslo on June 15, 1938, and were due to travel back in September. However, in consultation with their parents it was agreed that they should remain in Norway until further notice. At this point, the Oslo Board of Education saw to it that the children received Norwegian language instruction before they started attending a regular public school.[259] Josef Fenster, who entered class 2D, had experienced "der Anschluss" on March 12, 1938, the day Austria was annexed by the Third Reich. He had heard shouts of "Sieg Heil" and "Heil Hitler," as Jewish men were sent to clean the streets and sidewalks while they were kicked and mocked.[260] He told me that starting school at Majorstua was wonderful. On the night of November 26, 1942, the children were rescued and sent to Sweden by Nic. Waal and Gerda Tandberg, who evacuated the orphanage, then located on Holbergs gate.[261]

During the summer of 1939, Kathe Lasnik traveled with Inger Becker and her brother, Kurt Becker, to a farm, which doubled as a private children's camp or boarding house. Inger Becker had been there before. The girls knew each other from the synagogue in Bergstien and from religion classes. Inger Becker lived in Løren in Østre Aker; her father ran a knitwear shop on Tøyengata, near Grønlandsleiret.[262] The girls took a train to the farm. Elise Lasnik accompanied her little sister on the journey and visited her on Sundays. The farmer picked the children up at the train station and drove them the last few kilometers in a horse and cart.

The farm was located on a hilltop in the district of Lunner between Hadeland and Jevnaker. A steep path led from the house down to a lake, where Kathe Lasnik and Inger Becker swam every day. The children accompanied the farmer when he brought the hay into the barn. They ate their meals in the farmhouse – supper was often served out on a large patio – but they lived in their own house. They shared a room with two other girls, and in the evenings before they slept, they talked about the meals and the farm and how their families in the city were doing.

Kathe Lasnik and Inger Becker wrote letters home. To mail them, they had to go to the store next to the train station, which could only be reached by traveling a couple of kilometers along a cart path that twisted through the hilly landscape. Kathe Lasnik and Inger Becker walked and talked about what they wanted to buy at the store, what they were going to do when they got back to the city, who was going to come to visit them on Sunday, and what they hoped to have for lunch.

Near the station, the path followed along the edge of a grove of trees. On the other side a field sloped down toward the train tracks.

One time, they stopped and remained standing. They had been talking about something that absorbed them, but it was not for that reason that they forgot everything else and came to a sudden standstill. Inger Becker could not remember what they had been talking about. Nor could she remember the name of either the farm or the farmer, something like Ner, Nergård, Nerbø – something along those lines. However, she clearly remembered the mood that day, and also that they had come to a sudden stop at exactly the same time and had remained standing still.[263]

When World War II broke out on September 1, 1939, Kathe Lasnik had just started sixth grade. Coal and coke were strictly rationed and a ban was immediately issued against driving private automobiles.[264] Panting horses pulled the bread from the baking factory on the Norabakken hill; just like before, brewery horses came with loads of ale from the brewery down in Pilestredet up towards Suhms gate; and even though the summer was winding down, the girls bicycled to Bygdøy to swim on warm afternoons.[265]

Elise Lasnik got engaged on New Year's Eve, 1939 – her birthday – to Julius Bassist. He was from Stockholm, but could not find work in Sweden and so had traveled to relatives in Oslo. He worked in a store. Elias and Dora Lasnik were not entirely pleased. Anna Lasnik was the second oldest and so it was her turn to be engaged.[266] In February, 1940, Elias Lasnik was admitted to Diakonissehuset's hospital. Simply going up stairs or inclines robbed him of breath. At the hospital, doctors discovered he was suffering from pulmonary emphysema and bronchitis. He was in the hospital for a couple of weeks and was posted for a follow-up on May 5.[267]

During the night of April 9, air-raid warning sirens went off at 12:15 a.m. and people sought their bomb shelters until the "danger over" signal sounded at 1:35 a.m. Hertzbergs gate 7 had a bomb shelter in the cellar, so the Lasnik family did not have far to go. At 4:20 a.m. the sirens again went off and this time the "danger over" signal did not sound until 6:20 a.m. The third time the Oslo population was forced to seek shelter was 7:30 a.m. Since German planes circled the city the rest of that day, the "danger over" signal never came.[268] As a result, school was cancelled on April 9.[269]

Early in the morning, Prime Minister Johan Nygaardsvold's cabinet met in the city of Hamar together with the Norwegian parliament and the monarchy. Oslo's Chief of Police, Kristian Welhaven, sent the traffic police chief, along with 40 men, to Skøyen to escort the German soldiers, who had landed at the airport in Fornebu, to Akershus Fortress. People lined the sidewalks and called out insults to the policemen.[270]

That evening Major Vidkun Quisling read his proclamation on the Norwegian Broadcasting Corporation's (NRK) radio program at 7:30 p.m. and 10:00 p.m.: "Because England has violated Norway's neutrality by laying minefields in Norwegian territory without meeting any resistance other than the usual feeble protests from the Nygaardsvold government, the German government has offered Norway armed assistance." Quisling also claimed that Nygaardsvold's government had "stepped down" and that a new national government with himself at its head "had taken control." The following day, the newspaper Lofotposten printed Quisling's radio speech with the heading: "German Dictatorship Introduced in Norway".[271]

Nygaardsvold's government had not, in fact, stepped down; but had been supplanted by councils from the Conservatives, Liberals and Farmers' Party, which at the parliament's last meeting at Elverum had assumed the power to act on parliament's behalf. It was there that the parliament had been dissolved and the representatives given the choice of either returning to the districts occupied by Hitler's Germany or following the government northwards.

On April 10, therefore, the bomb shelter at Hertzbergs gate 7 was packed. It was not only the building's residents who sought shelter there. Edith Gjeruldsen, one of Kathe Lasnik's friends, also came with her parents. After all, the building they lived in across the street did not have a cellar that could be used as a bomb shelter. Late in the morning, they received word that they should come out to where a few trucks were waiting in the street. In the jostling that followed,

Kathe Lasnik was separated from her parents and placed in the same truck as Edith Gjeruldsen and her parents.

The truck was carrying eggs and milk, and had been in the process of delivering its wares to the dairies at Majorstua when it was requisitioned. In order to make room for passengers, most of the milk and eggs were thrown into the gutter. People were in a hurry to get away; there was a rumor that the city was going to be bombed at 12:00 p.m.

Edith Gjeruldsen and Kathe Lasnik seized onto an equally gruesome rumor: The Germans were going to transport hundreds of corpses from the German warship Blücher, which had been sunk near Drøbak, through Oslo and no one was allowed to see the dead German soldiers. It was for this reason that people were being chased out of the city. The truck drove out to Sognsvann Lake. After that, they trudged the five kilometers to Ullevålseter through slush and snow. Many people arrived at the popular ski lodge during the course of the day. The adults sat and talked together. Sometime during the evening, Kathe Lasnik and Edith Gjeruldsen lay down under a table and tried to sleep. The following afternoon, the company headed west to Nordmarka, to Tryvann, and then down into Sørkedalen. They returned to the city by bus.[272]

Anna Lasnik and Elise Lasnik had ended up in Østmarka, while Elias and Dora Lasnik did not go anywhere, and so were home at Hertzbergs gate on "panic day."[273] For their part, Leopold and Jenny Bermann, along with their small son, did not want to risk remaining in Norway. With this in mind, they arrived in Røros on April 26, 1940, and the District Sheriff stamped their passports before they crossed the border to Malmagen, Sweden.[274] After that, the family traveled to Stockholm, sought out the Norwegian legate, and secured an extension on their passports until May 27, 1941. Jenny Bermann[275] and her son stayed in the Refugee Home in Södertälje just outside of Stockholm, while Leopold Bermann stayed in the Norwegian Home at Linnéagatan 20, in order to make it easier for him to look for work and housing opportunities in Sweden.[276]

The teacher's council at Majorstua School recorded in its minutes that "[b]ecause of the German's incursion into the country on 9/4 and the resulting occupation, Majorstua School is closed until 26/4-40."[277] The occupiers seized the school on April 15, intending to quarter soldiers there. At first, the students were sent to Bolteløkka School, but when that school also became a soldiers' barracks, classes were held at the homes of teachers and parents, in churches, meeting houses, or movie theaters. Class 6C was held in the home of Miss Rønnaug Heyerdahl Larsen on Industrigaten 11 in the Frogner district.[278]

Turid Ekestrand, who lived at Schultz' gate 6, went home with Kathe Lasnik from Miss Heyerdahl Larsen's apartment to do her homework. Since her father was taking part in the campaign against the Wehrmacht, Turid Ekestrand had traveled together with her mother and sisters to a house the family had in Ringerike. She had taken schoolbooks with her so she could continue with her lessons, but unfortunately the house burnt down with her school books in it. Therefore, Turid Ekestrand did not have schoolbooks when she came to the city at the beginning of May, and so went home with Kathe Lasnik. They sat together in the maid's room. Dora Lasnik brought cake – sometimes cream cake – to the industrious girls.[279]

14

A Strange Logic

INFLUENTIAL GERMANS QUICKLY understood that Vidkun Quisling's coup on April 9 would only lead to increased Norwegian resistance. As a result, Quisling was removed on April 15 in favor of a civil administration of Norwegian officials, who would manage the German-occupied territories. In the meantime, Josef Terboven came to Oslo on April 21, and on April 24 he was named National Commissioner, a post directly answerable to Adolf Hitler, and was given dictatorial authority. Accordingly, the "Reich Commissariat for the Occupied Norwegian Territories" moved into the Parliament Building to ensure that the civil administration, which acted through the administrative council, carried out orders issued by the occupying German authority.[280]

On May 10 or 11, the police arrived at Hertzbergs gate 7 to confiscate the Lasnik family's radio.[281] It was seized in accordance with a directive issued by Detective Wilhelm Esser, who had visited Oslo police headquarters with a list of all the Jews who owned radios. The list was incomplete, however, so a police inspector, aided by Telegrafverket, the state-operated telecommunications monopoly, among others, drew up new lists. As a result, 107 radios were seized in Oslo and Aker municipalities.[282]

On the heels of this activity, the administrative council demanded an explanation from the Oslo Police Chief, Kristian Welhaven: Why, they asked, had he complied with the German request without contacting anyone? District recorder Harbeck undertook the task of interrogating the police chief. During the interrogation, Kristian

Welhaven maintained that it would have been of no use to protest, since the police did not have "[p]ermission to resist such an order." In any case, it was better to "convince the Germans that in Norway there was no reason to take such actions against the Jews."[283]

Harbeck found this to be a strange logic: How was one supposed to keep the Germans from doing something by following their orders to the letter? He contacted Hans Dellbrügge in the National Commissariat, but was immediately turned away: the Jewish question was an international affair. As a result, Harbeck's protest produced no results, something he attributed to the fact that the radios had already been confiscated.[284] .

Around the same time, in the middle of May, 1940, the Jewish religious communities in Oslo and Trondhjem were ordered to compile lists of their members' names, birth dates, occupation, and addresses. The Norwegian police had asked the religious communities for these lists, but the Germans had ordered the police to do it. In August, the religious communities were further asked to provide lists of Jews who were not members.[285] By this time, the leadership of the Mosaic Religious Community had concluded that the Jews in Norway had nothing to fear so long as they did nothing to resist the new regime. Therefore, members should immediately comply with whatever they were asked to do, as compliance was undoubtedly the best protection against persecution and harassment. That was the strategy the Mosaic Religious Community pursued for as long as it continued to exist in Norway.[286]

An officer from the Criminal Police Department in Stockholm arrived at the beginning of July to inspect the people then living in the Norwegian Home. The Swedish policeman met with Leopold Bermann, who explained that he "intended to remain in the country until further notice." Since he did not have the "appropriate residence permit," however, he was asked to go to the National Board of Health and Welfare,[287] where he received a form and applied for a residence permit that would be valid in Sweden until May 27, 1941. Under "reason for visit," he wrote "refugee."[288] Jenny Bermann wrote the same thing on her form when she applied for a residence permit for herself and her son, also until May 27, 1941.[289]

While Leopold and Jenny Bermann were in Sweden, Elias Lasnik was again hospitalized. However, they did not discover anything that they did not already know, and concluded that he had perhaps had a case of tuberculosis that had healed by itself. He was discharged until Midsummer's Day.[290]

The day after the Aliens Office in Sweden had received the Bermanns' residence permit applications, the office wrote to the Over-Governor's Office in order to arrange a hearing for Leopold and Jenny Bermann.[291] However, when Detective Carl E. Palm arrived to interview Leopold Bermann, all he could determine was that the man had already left. Leopold Bermann had already moved to the Refugee Home in Södertälje on July 7,[292] where the couple again discussed what they should do. As a result, on July 11, 1940, the Swedish authorities in Eda stamped "departed" on the couple's passports and, on the Norwegian side, Magnor customs officials acknowledged that their baggage had been inspected. Finally, the German Border Police in Magnor stamped their passports and documented that the couple had traveled back into Norway.[293]

Leopold and Jenny Bermann were not the only people to return from Sweden after the initial events of the war were over. After August, however, the German occupiers refused to grant entrance to the Jews who had fled to Sweden.[294] Before that, though, many people traveled home to Norway because the situation seemed stable. In addition, the Swedish authorities did not always seem very welcoming.

In 1940, Anna Lasnik had a turnover of 40,000 kroner in Markveien Kitchen Supplies. Her take-home income was 2,149 kroner.[295] On her tax return for 1940, Elise Lasnik wrote in the space reserved for dependents that she and Anna Lasnik supported her father, mother and one sister. Therefore, she asked if the basic tax deductions they were entitled to "could be split between Anna Lasnik and myself."[296]

In the fall of 1940, Principal Thorstein Kvarre informed the teachers at Majorstua School about the schedule, materials and schoolbooks for the new school year. In the afternoon, students would be sent to Uranienborg School, where instruction would continue. In the September teachers' meeting, recess and class inspection were addressed, as well as the "handling and use of blackout curtains."[297] During November 1940, the head teacher also introduced a few new regulations: "1) quick entrance, 2) follow the class to the door, 3) make sure the doors are closed, 4) bathroom inspections." Furthermore, there were "instructions on the winter schedule and on air raid alarm procedure."[298] New teachers were assigned for the last elementary school year of class 7C: newly graduated Elna Marie Hauger took over from Rønnaug Heyerdahl Larsen, who retired with a pension, Miss Gjertrud Lorange would teach English, and Miss Hoel home economics.[299]

After a while, children and parents began to notice that it was at night around the full moon that the air raid sirens were most likely to go off. As a result, the children began sleeping in their clothes, so that they could get down to the bomb shelters more quickly. Since the school did not have a good bomb shelter, they used the tunnel for the underground subway. While people were waiting for the "danger over" signal, they would use the dark tunnel to get from one place in the city to another.[300]

The parents complained to the school regarding afternoon instruction: wasn't it possible to switch the schedule from afternoon to morning?[301] For many of the students in 7C, the trek from Uranienborg School was not actually any longer than the one from Majorstua School. The way the afternoon instruction had been set up, however, forced them to traverse a blacked-out city during the fall and winter.[302]

During a teachers' meeting held at the beginning of February, 1941, attention was drawn to a document from the Ministry "with orders to attend the Hitler Youth Exhibition and [they were] told that classes 5-7 from Majorstua" had to attend the event on Thursday, February 11, 1941.[303] However, none of the students from 7C can remember ever having gone. I found an explanation for this in a report from Sinsen High School. Sinsen had requested that attendance be made voluntary, rather than mandatory. The Ministry denied their request. Still, teachers and students refused to go; it had been agreed that students would simply not show up for school. At a meeting at Sinsen, this idea was explained to a hundred representatives from the other schools in Oslo and Aker, who all decided to do the same thing, and so the exhibition was effectively boycotted.[304]

In the meantime, Principal Kvarre thought it was necessary to make "a serious request to the staff to be very careful about what they said." Furthermore, "[t]he children should be told to leave posters alone, and they should not harass their peers."[305] Nonetheless, students turned their backs on members of the Norwegian Fascist Party, the Nasjonal Samling (NS),[306] and Helga Brun in Kathe Lasnik's class received appreciative looks from the teacher when she slammed the classroom window shut as singing German soldiers marched by.[307]

On May 17, 1941, the Swedish journalist Curt Falkenstam wrote a report on the mood in Norway. The public could see right through the censored press, he believed, and the Norwegian people read newspapers in a particular way: "Things that are talked up are seen as inconsequential and vice versa." A German senior official further explained to the Swedish journalist why the NS's membership numbers were not made public. "Compared to the [total] population, it would make a terrible impression [...] from a pure propaganda standpoint." According to the figures to which Curt Falkenstam had access, the NS's membership numbers hovered somewhere between 30,000 and 40,000 individuals.[308]

Just after the Swedish journalist's article was printed in the Swedish newspaper *Stockholms Tidningen*, Heinrich Himmler visited Norway to swear in a new division of SS soldiers. In doing so, Himmler admonished the Norwegian soldiers: "We march towards the future as a National Socialist organization, in accordance with the immutable race laws. We hope and trust that we are not just the few who fight for this good cause, but that we are the founding fathers of the tribe that is necessary for the future of the Germanic people."[309]

15

Kathe Lasnik Takes Her Elementary School Exam

1939 WAS THE first year that collective examination was introduced into the Oslo school system. Since it had not been possible to administer the test in 1940, however, the School Board had decided that in 1941 the exam should be held as usual. The exams would be corrected by a male and a female teacher. Examination would take place on June 17.

The subject choices for the Norwegian composition portion were written on the board:

What I'll never forget

A day during vacation

Imagine that you travel from Oslo to Japan. Describe your trip

The number of students who chose the first two exercises was about equal, but only ten percent wrote about an imaginary trip to Japan. Of those students who chose to write about an unforgettable experience, 70 percent wrote about tragic and unpleasant things. For the most part, students who wrote about the war focused on the night of April 9 and on "panic day." In doing so, they were describing their experience of serious war events and evacuation.[310]

In 7C, 11 students received an M (very good), 12 got a G (good), and four got an NG (average) in Norwegian composition. Kathe got a G, the same as her final grade in the subject.[311]

The English exam consisted of 17 questions that had to be answered "in complete sentences." The first question was "What is the blackboard made of?" and the last was "What is the use of the lungs?" These questions were followed by a rewriting exercise from active to passive voice, the numbers from one to 14 to be written out, and a sentence that had to be conjugated for all persons in the present tense.[312] Kathe got a G (good) on this text, which was again her final grade in this subject.[313]

The last day of the exam was math. The math test had two parts. The first involved calculation, while the second concerned practical arithmetic. When grades were assigned, the fact was taken into account that boys and girls had not had the same number of class hours devoted to math and certainly had not had the same curriculum.

The first and simplest question on the math test was: "There were 215 apples in one box and 100 in another box. There were 9 apples in every kg. How many kg. of apples were there?" The most difficult question was nr. 24: "For every 10 steps Rolf traveled 5 m. and Lars 8. Rolf took 14 steps in 6 seconds, and Lars 10 steps in 6 seconds. Both were walking from Oslo to Kikut. Lars started half an hour later than Rolf, but when he was halfway to Kikut, he passed Rolf. What was the distance between Oslo and Kikut?" Hardly anyone answered it correctly.

The practical exercise was about a ski club that had bought some land in order to build a cabin. The students had to figure out what the cabin would cost.[314]

Kathe Lasnik received an M (very good) as her final grade in math, though on the exam she got an S (excellent). In total, there were seven in the class who ended up with M as their final grade, though everyone got an S on the exam. That S looked very good among all the Gs (good) on her report card. She also got an M in handiwork and in spoken Norwegian; otherwise, she received a G in history, geography, science, writing and drawing. Like her older sisters, she did not receive an especially good grade in culture-related subjects.[315]

Photograph hanging next to the bronze relief memorial at Fagerborg School.

DISSE ELEVER AV
FAGERBORG SKOLE
GAV SITT LIV FOR NORGE
I KRIGEN 1940-1945

ARNE KRISTIAN MYKLEBOST ✦ ISAK KRUPP
KAARE HAGEN ✦ HALLSTEIN BARDI VALLDAL
ERNST ARMIN FYRWALD ✦ PAUL BERNSTEIN
MARTIN FEINBERG ✦ NORMAN MORRIS RIUNG
OSCAR ALBERT LÜTKEN ✦ BENJAMIN GARMI
BJØRN LORNTSNER ✦ KÄTHE RITA LASNICK
ROLF JUUL HENNINGSEN ✦ ESTHER KARPOL
KNUT LINDAAS ✦ TRYGVE EIRIK SVINDLAND
JAN EIGIL LØFSGAARD ✦ HERMANN FEINBERG
BERNT BARGE ✦ FRANTZ PHILIP HOPSTOCK
MAURITZ PLESANSKY ✦ JAN ERLING HEIDE
RACHEL FEINBERG ✦ ABRAHAM JOSEF ARSCH
TOR GREINER STENERSEN ✦ PER LINDÅAS
GUNNAR KROGSBØL ✦ OLA CHRISTOPHERSEN
PETER KRISTIAN YOUNG ✦ KJELL DOBKES
FRITZ JØRG. O. HVAM ✦ PETER CHRISTIAN RING
AAGE FRITZ STUBBERØD ✦ HÅKON LAKSOV
PER JACOBSEN ✦ HALVOR SVERRE RØDAAS
BJØRN HILT ✦ JAAMPA KROG ✦ JAKOB FRIIS

KATHE – R – LASNIK
F. 13 – 10 – 1927

Memorial plaque at the Jewish cemetery, Helsfyr, Oslo. Photo: Siri Boquist.

The bronze relief at Fagerborg School was made by Principal Simes at the Oslo National Academy of the Arts. Two students were arrested while attending Fagerborg School during the war: Rachel Feinberg and Kathe Lasnik. Photo: K. Teigen.

LASNIK, KATHE RITA, gymnasiast, Oslo. Født 13. oktober 1927 i Oslo, datter av Elias Lasnik, f. 1887 i Vilna, og Dora f. Meszansky, f. 1888 s. st. Ble arrestert under jødeforfølgelsene i Norge og ført til Tyskland 26. november 1942 sammen med foreldre og en søster. Ved ankomsten til Auschwitz i desember s. å. ble hun straks sendt i gasskammer.

Entry in *Vår Falne* (*Our Fallen*), a commemorative four-volume set of books published by the Norwegian government in 1949-51.

The *Donau*, which departed from Utstikker in Oslo on November 26, 1942, with 532 Jews on board. Photo: Norway's Resistance Museum.

Aar	Dag	Gade	Nr.	Etg.	Opg	Anmerkning
08	1/2	Rusland				
09	1/2	Thv. Meyers g	26	1	2	
"	21/3	Grüners gt.	5	2	1	
"	1/11	Markvn	26	2	bg	
12	26/8	Wilses gt.	6	1	1	
15	1/2	—"—	6	3	1	
27	1/8	—"—	6	4	1	egen ...
36	4	**Fredensborgvn.**	2	3	1	e. l.
38	15/12	Hertzbergsg.	7	1	b	e. l
43	1/12	Ukjent		opg av	Thv Hasund
42	26/11	deportert med	d/s	Donau		
		ifl. liste mottatt gj...				

Excerpt from Elias Lasnik's registration card, Population Registry, the Regional State Archives in Oslo. The addresses listed are circled on the map.

Oslo before World War II

Oslo Survey Department, 1938. Scale 1:15000

MÅLESTOKK 1:15000

100   0   100   200   300   400   500 M

Above: Fredensborgveien 2. The family lived in the apartment on the left-hand side of the third floor from April 1936 until December 1938

Left: The Lasnik family lived at Wilses gate 6 for 24 years, from 1912 to 1936. First they lived on the first floor and operated a fruit shop to the right of the gateway. From 1913 to 1927 the family lived on the third floor, and from 1927 to 1936 on the fourth floor, behind the three windows on the far left.

Hertzbergs gate 7. Kathe Lasnik lived in the apartment on the first floor with the white balcony from December 15, 1938, until she was arrested on November 26, 1942. The street is named after theologian Niels Hertzberg (1759-1841), one of the signers of the Norwegian Constitution. In 1841 he supported Henrik Wergeland's battle to rescind the so-called Jewish clause, which prohibited the immigration of Jews into Norway, and explained why he had voted in favor of it originally: "Like so many thoughtless youngsters I harbored a sort of distaste for the Jews, which I had unfortunately imbibed with my mother's milk; for I had from my childhood years heard that Jews should not live in Norway, because they would take over the Kongsberg Silver Mines and carry all the silver out of the country..." All photos on this page: Siri Boquist.

Bridesmaid, November 7, 1937, at the wedding of Jenny Lasnik and Leopold Bermann. Photo: private collection.

Kathe Lasnik with her little nephew. Photo: private collection.

Kathe Lasnik squints in the sharp spring sunlight during an outing in 1940. Between Kathe Lasnik and Jenny Bermann is Ivar Bermann. Photo: private collection.

Fagerborg girls on bicycles. From left: Kathe Lasnik, Anita Østern and Ingrid Prytz, probably spring of 1941. Photo: private collection.

Fagerborg girls with bouquets of anemones, probably spring of 1941. From left: Kathe Lasnik, Anita Østern, Bjørg Tutta Hansen and Berit Hofsgaard. Photo: private collection.

Near Hertzbergs gate 3. Standing from left: Bjørg Tutta Hansen Anita Østern, Kjell Jensen (behind), Ingrid Prytz, Kathe Lasnik, Anne-Lise Christiansen and Kari Harseth. The boys sitting in the front are Henning Skoglund and Tore Skotner. Spring 1941. Photo: private collection

In the country. From left: Jenny Bermann, Ivar Bermann, Elias Lasnik, Anna Lasnik, Kathe Lasnik and Dora Lasnik. Summer 1939. Photo: private collection.

Class 7C, Majorstua School, in front of Middelthuns gate 11, June 1941, after the elementary school exams. Bottom row: Inger Lise Schou, Ella Winter-Petersen, Celia Century. 2nd row: Turid Eskestrand, Aud Holmsen, Dagny Alexander, Märtha Lütken, Rigmor Schrøder, Rigmor Kopstad. 3rd row: Solveig Krosby, Kathe Lasnik, Ruth Gundersen, Margrethe Jensen, Astri Heiberg, Randi Elton, Helga Brun. Top row: Liv Nilsen, Janiske Didrichsen, Berit Monen, Britt Finne, Randi Aronsen. Photo: private collection.

Berit Hofgaard took a picture of her friends, who were playing. Photo: private collection.

Left: Anita Østern and Kathe Lasnik (behind), Bjørg Tutta Hansen and Berit Hofgaard (in front) while on a trip to the forest with the Østern family, probably spring of 1940. Photo: private collection.

Summer 1941. From left: Ivar Bermann, Elise Lasnik, Julius Bassist, Kathe Lasnik, unknown, Anna Lasnik, Elias Lasnik and Jenny Bermann Photo: private collection.

Pictures taken in the fall of 1942. The photos on this and the previous pages are the only pictures of Kathe Lasnik that have been found, and all were taken between 1937 and 1941 or 1942. Photos: private collection.

Homeroom teacher Norvald Greina put a question mark in the margin when Kathe Lasnik had been arrested and did not come to school on November 26, 1942.

~ [7   *Lasnik, Kathe Rita*

Til Tutta

Heia, Tutt, du må ikke
være lei
Snart har du nok en mann
gående og titte på deg
Jeg vet at du ikke blir lykkelig
sinna gammel kone.
Jeg håber du blir lykkelig.
med en mann selv uten krone
Kathe
Lasnik

Astri,
du evner har
flink på skolen du alltid var.
Leksene du alltid kunde.
selv om du ofte måtte skunde.

Rundt i verden du har fart
og lært mye rart.
Lykke på din vei du må få
og fremtidens riktige vei må gå!

3/5-41.   Kathe Lasnik.

Two poems that Kathe Lasnik wrote in autograph albums, or poetry albums as they were called then, have been kept. She wrote in an album belonging to Bjørg Hansen, who was called Tutta and lived in Suhms gate 3. Her father was a janitor.

The second poem was for Astri Heiberg in class 7C at Majorstua School. She lived in Hertzbergs gate 24 B. Astri Heiberg was the daughter of stockbroker Gustav Heiberg, and her mother was English. Astri was born in England and lived in New York until she was five years old.

Elias and Dora Lasnik with Jenny, probably 1911. He was an apprentice tinsmith and she worked in a tobacco factory. Photo: private collection.

Kathe Lasnik's sisters: Elise Lasnik (born 1913), Anna Lasnik (born 1911) and Jenny Lasnik (born 1909). Photo: private collection.

Municipal census form filled out by Elias Lasnik, February 1, 1910.

Spørreskjema

for

jøder i Norge

fra

Oslo .... politidistrikt.

Etternavn .... *Lasnik*
(For kvinner også pikenavnet)

Samtlige fornavn .... *Kathe Rita*
(Bruksnavnet understrekes)

Født (sted, datum, år) *13/10-24 Oslo* .... I hvilket land *Norge*

Privatadr. (gt., nr., by) *Herzbergsgt. 4 b I. Oslo*
.... Privattlf.

Nuværende religionssamfund *Mosaiske* .... Siden når *Siden fødselen*

Tidligere religionssamfund ....

Familieforhold: (Ugift, gift, enkestand, skilt) *Ugift*

For- og etternavn på ektefellen ....
(For kvinner pikenavnet)

Ektefellens fødested, datum og år ....

Har ektefellen jødisk innslag i familien? ....

Antall barn: ....

(Navn)   (Alder)   (Oppholdssted)

....

Nuværende erhvervsyrke *Skoleelev* .... Selvstendig? ~~Ja~~/Nei

Yrke av fag ....

Event. biyrker ....

Teoretisk og praktisk utdannelse ....

Militær utdannelse ....

Offentlige tillitshverv ....

Medl. av fagl. organisasjoner før ....

Medl. av fagl. organisasjoner nu ....

Medl. av andre foreninger og organisasjoner ....

Har De vært frimurer? *nei* Fra .... til ....

Hvilken grad? .... Hverv ....

Nasjonalitet *Norsk* .... Statsborgerskap *Norsk*

Når kom De til Norge *Alltid vært i Norge*

Siste oppholdssted utenfor Norge ....

2. 42. nelson trykk, oslo

Sigfried Nylander at the National Unification Party's Office of Statistics planned to establish a Jewish index card file, and began by drawing up a "Questionnaire for Jews in Norway" that was to be filled out by everyone with a "J" stamp in their identity papers. The questionnaires were used by the State Police when arresting Jews in Oslo. After the war, Nylander claimed that "the statistical work was carried out on a purely professional basis, and I did not participate in the political work, nor was I a member of any committee or commission; the calculations and statistics were only assessed according to the forms that were sent in or collected."

Elias Lasnik's tinsmith workshop was located at Brogaten 6 from 1933 onwards. It was in one of the annexes in the courtyard. Photo: Oslo City Museum, 1936.

Dora Lasnik's signature on the form listing confiscated assets, October 26, 1942.

The last picture taken of Elias and Dora Lasnik, in the summer of 1942 (the photo has been cropped). Photo: private collection.

Elise Lasnik married Julius Bassist in
Stockholm on November 29, 1942.
Photo: private collection.

Jewish women being chased into gas chamber V. The photo was probably taken in 1944 by a Greek Jew. Photo:
Auschwitz-Birkenau State Museum.

General map of Birkenau, showing the railroad tracks where the Norwegian Jews arrived on December 1, 1942. The hatched area beside the tracks shows the platform where men between the ages of 15 and 60 who could work were separated from the women, children and elderly. The men were then marched to Auschwitz, where they were registered, while the women and children were transported in trucks in the opposite direction. The railroad tracks into the camp were first used in May 1944.

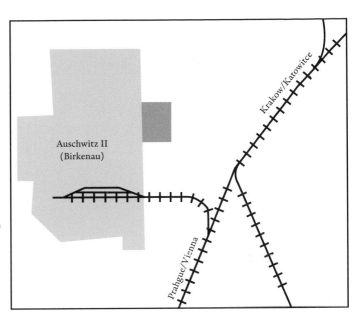

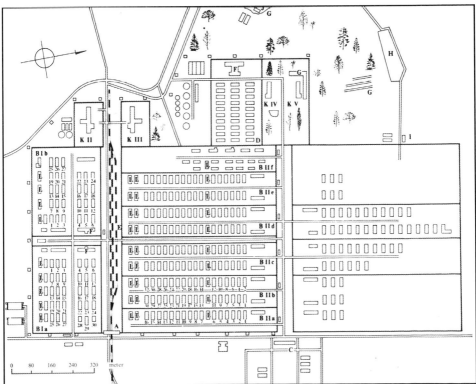

In December 1942 there were two gas chambers (I and J) in Birkenau. It has not been determined to which of these the Norwegian Jews were taken. The gas chambers with crematoria (K II, III, IV and V) were built later. The corpses from the provisional gas chambers were dragged outside and burned on the ground (G).

Sources: Franciczek Piper: *Die Zahl der Opfer von Auschwitz*, Oswiecim 1993. Teresa Swilebocka: *Auschwitz, A History in Photographs*, Oswiecim, 1993. Danuta Czech: *Kalendarium der Ereignisse im Konzentrationslager Auschwitz-Birkenau 1939-45*, Hamburg 1989

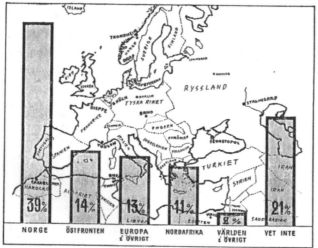

BÅTEN MED JUDAR FRÅN NORGE
ÅRETS HÄNDELSE FÖR DE FLESTA.

39% NORGE — **14%** ÖSTFRONTEN — **13%** EUROPA i ÖVRIGT — **11%** NORDAFRIKA — **8 %** VÄRLDEN i ÖVRIGT — **21%** VET INTE

On New Year's Eve, 1943, the front page of the newspaper *Dagens Nyheter* printed a graph showing the answers collated by the Swedish Gallup Institute for the question: "What foreign affairs event from 1942 do you think will be remembered best?" The headline reads: "The boat with Jews from Norway was the event of the year for the largest number of people." The countries or regions listed, from the left: Norway, the Eastern Front, Europe and other, North Africa, the world and other, don't know. Facsimile: All over press, Norway.

Knut Rød during his trial in April, 1948. Photo: NTB (the Norwegian News Agency).

Policemen and police officers photographed after a study trip to Berlin in 1942. Photo: Tom. B. Jensen.

16

A Reconciliation in Advance

JUST AFTER THE girls in class 7C held their farewell party at Helga Brun's apartment at Middelthunsgate 11,[316] a new police force was established in Norway: the State Police or Stapo. The Stapo would be a special police division that dealt with "espionage, rebellion, sabotage, refugee matters, illegal newspapers and so on."[317] Stapo was combined with the police surveillance divisions and by the fall of 1941 consisted of 150 men. Karl A. Martinsen, who had been trained as a non-commissioned officer and who had joined the NS in the fall of 1940, was named chief. The occupying German authorities gave orders directly to the Stapo. With the exception of five people, everyone in the Stapo was a member of the NS.[318]

After the Norwegian forces had surrendered in Norway on June 10, 1940, negotiations were started between the National Commissariat and the parliamentary presidency to transform the Administrative Council into a National Council for the whole country. These negotiations broke down on September 18, 1940, and a week later Josef Terboven appointed commissarial ministers, each of whom had charge of a Ministry and was answerable to him.[319] The Stapo was placed under the Ministry of the Police, which was headed by commissarial minister Jonas Lie.

The day that Kathe Lasnik received her elementary school report card, June 22, 1941, Hitler's Germany attacked the Soviet Union. The following day, Adolf Gorvitz, Elias Lasnik's tinsmith colleague, and 63 other stateless Eastern European Jews were arrested and interred in Grini. In northern Norway (Nord-Norge), every Jewish man was arrested; in Trøndelag only 12.[320] At the beginning of July, Adolf Gorvitz and most of the others were released.[321] German troops captured Vilna on July 4, 1941, and immediately began executing Jews with the willing help of Lithuanian policemen and Fascists.[322] Elise Lasnik went to the Theatercafé with her fiancé, Julius Bassist, even though it was crawling with German officers. Through relatives, Julius Bassist was also able to obtain eggs and others rationed foodstuffs for his future mother-in-law. However, she usually gave them to her oldest daughter, so that her small son would get enough to eat.[323] In August 1941, when Hitler's divisions had conquered the better part of what had been known as "Yiddishland," Kathe Lasnik started middle school.

Hertzbergs gate was part of the Fagerborg public school district, where school fees amounted to 200 kroner per year.[324] Since the financial records are gone, however, it is no longer possible to determine whether or not Kathe Lasnik had a tuition waiver. In the meantime, Fagerborg School also functioned as a German soldiers' barracks, so the students and teachers met at Vestheim School, which was located near the end of Bygdøy Allé. Twelve boys and 14 girls started class 1D with Kathe Lasnik.

Eight of the girls in 1D had also been in class 7C at Majorstua School.[325] Of the eight, one apparently immigrated to the USA, another did not remember anything of importance, and three could not be located. That leaves three more. One of them told me that she and Kathe Lasnik had been sledding in Stensparken. It had been a Wednesday and they had hugged each other before parting. To this day she believes that the hug was a form of reconciliation, that it was Kathe Lasnik's expression of forgiveness for what was to come, a farewell, because they knew they would be parted. That hug has become a central event in her life.

Norvald Greina was the homeroom teacher for 1D. He had majored in English and had written a thesis in 1922 on the Scottish historian Thomas Carlyle.[326] According to the teachers' council's meeting minutes from the fall of 1941, he and his colleagues had quite a bit to contend with. As they noted about various students: "is disobedient and should report to school early as a reprimand," "interrupts with talking," "out – reported," "does math homework [...] during religious instruction classes," "sits there with unimportant things during English instruction. Warned," "cheats in history, has ripped a page out of the book and sits with it between his other papers," "is rude and ought to be reprimanded," "rips out the pages that the lesson is on and copies during written test[s]," "writes German rote lessons from Monday, has not studied," "whispers during history instruction, a couple of others were warned before," "says he does not have the parent-teacher communication booklet at all. Reprimand!", "cheats in math, grade T in behavior," "interrupts with talking," "ought to be reprimanded more than once, since he disturbs instruction," "ought to be reprimanded, since he doesn't pay attention and disturbs the student who sits behind him."[327]

According to the reform instituted in 1936, students continuing their education would start middle school after seven years of elementary school, and could attend a third year of high school after the first two. As a result, Norvald Greina subjected his class to a rigorous evaluation. On the first report card, two students got an M (very good), 14 a T (satisfactory), two an NG (average), four an MG (barely passing), and three an Ikke (failing). Kathe Lasnik was one of the four who got an MG. The transition from elementary school had been difficult, but when the next report cards were issued in October, November, and December, she received a T.[328]

When the teachers' council assessed Norvald Greina's class, 1D, on December 15, 1941, it was noted that eight of the 25 students probably should not have been there at all.

17

"J" Stamp

JOSEF TERBOVEN DECLARED martial law on September 10, 1941. On the previous day, he had received a visit from the notorious Reinhard Heydrich, Himmler's right hand. Martial law meant that there was a ban against disturbing the peace of the workplace and a curfew between 8:00 p.m. and 5:00 a.m.; that all means of transport, with the exception of rail, should stop at 7:00 p.m.; that there was a ban against selling and serving alcoholic beverages; and that all public locales and restaurants had to close at 7:30 p.m. Dancing was also prohibited, movies and theaters were forced to close and gatherings of people were prohibited. As was printed in the NS newspaper *Fritt Folk*, any and all resistance would be "met by force of arms."[329] Two hundred people were arrested, most of them from labor movements. The Norwegian Confederation of Trade Unions' legal advisor, Viggo Hansteen, and the head of the union at the Skabo Railway Car Factory, Rolf Wickstrøm, were court-martialed and shot at Øster Rifle Club's shooting range at Stig, near Årvoll, outside of Oslo.[330]

On October 10, 1941, the Ministry of the Police received a letter from Heinrich Fehlis, chief of the German Security Police in Norway. He instructed the Ministry to ensure that all Jewish identification papers were marked with a red letter "J." As a result, towards the end of November the head of the security police, Oliver Møystad, and criminal chief Jørgen Wiermyhr sketched "J"s on a desk calendar. Indeed, they tried out three different "J"s on the back of the page for Thursday, November 27, 1941. One was five, one was three, and one was two centimeters high. Eventually, they decided that a two-centimeter-high "J" was acceptable, so on December 20 the head of the security police, who acted for the Ministry of the Police, ordered "700 pcs. stamps" from the stamp factory Johs. Krogstie A/S, Stempelfabrik & Gravøranstalt, Storgaten 9, Oslo, and requested that the order "be executed as soon as possible."[331]

Already by January 5, Johs. Krogstie A/S was able to send 700 stamps at 67 øre each, along with an invoice for 496 kroner, to the Ministry of the Police.[332] And on January 13, the Ministry of the Police asked "the honorable" Ministry of Finance to pay this bill "according to Chapter 381-7B through Norges Bank to Johs. Krogstie A/S 469 kr. for the delivery of 700 stamps."[333]

When Jews brought their identification papers to their local police station, the stamps would be affixed.[334] At the same time, the Ministry of the Police collaborated with Heinrich Fehlis on an announcement. The Norwegian police, it seems, were confused about who exactly should receive stamps, because "according to Norwegian understanding," a Jew was "first and foremost [....] all members of the Mosaic Religious Community. And furthermore, all people of pure Jewish heritage (both parents of Jewish descent)." One note reads: "The main difficulties are solved if we limit the stamping requirement to all members of the mosaic religious community. As long as we do that, we can count on the compliance of the mosaic religious community and we can avoid having to advertise."[335] However, this definition was not acceptable to Heinrich Fehlis, and on November 22 he sent the Ministry of the Police the exact wording that he wished to be used, which included both members of the Mosaic Religious Community and those who were of Jewish heritage. "The directive concerning the stamping of identification papers for Jews" was sent out from the Ministry of the Police on January 10, 1942, to the police chiefs and district sheriffs. When the stamp was affixed, the police chief should also stamp "the index card [used for] proof of identification," since in this way "a complete list of Jews" could be drawn up in every district.[336]

Kathe Lasnik took her ID card with her picture, name, and address, and received a "J" stamp at the police department on Schultz' gate. Afterwards, she went over to Edith Gjeruldsen's and showed her the ID card, obviously insulted. She asked her friend why it should be only her ID that was stamped. She had not been frightened or worried, but rather indignant and affronted.[337]

Independently of Heinrich Fehlis's directive concerning the stamping of Jewish ID cards, the Nasjonal Samling's Statistics Office had taken its own initiatives. The agency was directed by Sigfried Nylander, who had single-handedly drawn up "lists of the Jewish firms in Norway as of December 1941,"[338] and then sent multiple copies of the list to NS County Governors, which could then be forwarded to district chiefs and updated. In a memo, he further noted that Haugesund Clothing Factory had been taken over by the NS and that "the Jew Rabinowitz [was] removed." Neither Markveien Kitchen Supplies nor Trondhjemsveien Kitchen Supplies was included on the list. The two small shops were probably not useful in lending credence to the idea of global economic domination.[339]

Sigfried Nylander also planned to establish a "Jewish card-index file."[340] Born in Sweden in 1891, he was the son of a doctor, had been a member of the Young Swedish Union, and had participated in the legendary Farmers' Train, when 50,000 farmers traveled to Stockholm and demanded that King Gustav strengthen the country's defenses. When he graduated from the institute of technology, Sigfried Nylander had wanted to go abroad and study in the USA. However, he remained trapped in the Norwegian city of Bergen on account of the U-boat blockade of 1917. He joined the NS in 1934.

Sigfried Nylander also drew up the "Questionnaire for Jews in Norway." He then sent a draft to the Ministry of the Police for commentary. Indeed, according to Jørgen Wiemyhr's summary on behalf of the Head of the State Criminal Police: "The initiative to register Jews in Norway [...] was taken by the Nasjonal Samling's Statistics Agency and exclusively by them without pressure on the part of the Germans."[341] On February 6, 1942, the NS Statistics Office ordered

12,000 copies of the questionnaire from Nelson Trykk, Kongensgt. 16, Oslo. The printer delivered the copies on February 21,[342] and Oliver Møystad and Jørgen Wiermyhr composed a cover letter to be sent to the police chiefs, who were then to make sure that three separate copies of the forms were filled out by everyone who had received a "J" stamp on their identification papers: one copy would go to the archives of the Ministry of the Police, one to the NS Statistics Office and one to the "Head of the Security Police"[343] in the Ministry of the Police. After the war, Nylander maintained that his statistics work "was purely professional" and that he did not participate "in police matters."[344]

At Hertzbergs gate 7, the Lasnik family filled out the "Questionnaire for Jews in Norway" on March 6, 1942.[345] Elise Lasnik filled out the questionnaire for both her parents. In response to the question about nationality, Elias and Dora both put "Russian," though they put "Norwegian" in response to the one about citizenship. Anna and Elise also filled out their own forms, while Kathe Lasnik did not fill out a form at all, since she was not yet fifteen years old.

18

An Intermezzo on Jacob Aalls Gate

AT THE SCHOOL council meeting directed by Principal Karl Aubert on January 28, 1942, it was noted that the "English national anthem and the royal anthem" should be omitted from English class until further notice. The last point Principal Karl Aubert addressed was concerning the extreme cold. Because of the inclement weather, students were staying in the corridors. Perhaps this was not such a bad thing, except for "the noise." Therefore, Fagerborg would follow the lead of Vestheim School and use "students from the upper classes to help take the students outside."[346]

Vidkun Quisling was named Norwegian Minister-President and formed a national Norwegian government on February 1, 1942. *Aftenposten* observed that this date was even more important in Norwegian history than May 17, 1814, the day the Constitution of Norway was signed at Eidsvoll, and June 7, 1905, the day Norway's union with Sweden was dissolved. One of the first measures Quisling took was to re-institute the repealed part of Article 2 of the Constitution from 1814 that stated: "Jews are prohibited from entry to the Realm," on March 12, 1942.[347]

The Ministry of Church Affairs and Education instructed all teachers to join the NS-led teachers' union. The organization would then prepare teachers for "their important assignment in the new state."[348] Although teachers who did not join had their salary frozen,[349] only 1,200 out of 14,000 teachers participated. Representatives of the new regime used the harsh winter and the fuel shortage as an excuse to close schools from February 28 until the beginning of May. To force more teachers to join the teachers' union, 1,100 teachers were arrested, and about 500 were sent with the steamer Skjærstad to the Norwegian town of Kirkenes, which the Germans used as a base during the war. Lars Dahle and Arnold Bekker from Fagerborg School were arrested.[350] Despite these measures, the Ministry of Church Affairs and Education made no headway with the teachers, and on April 25 the schools reopened. Fagerborg School had conducted sporadic instruction in private homes, but finally started up at the beginning of May, 1942, on the grounds of Foss School in Grünerløkka.[351] Principal Karl Aubert also wrote a letter to the Ministry of Church Affairs and Education: "We kindly request in the most urgent terms that the Ministry do whatever must be done so that the arrested teachers can be released as soon as possible. The Norwegian authorities' arrest of these teachers has horrified not only teachers, but also students and their parents." Principal Karl Aubert also noted that until "order is restored among the personnel by the release of the teachers, the school will not gain the confidence of the students' parents, which is necessary for a stable institution, and will not create that calm and security among the students that is the prerequisite for normal work. [...] We also allow ourselves to observe that instruction at a number of schools will be strongly affected, and that many schools can only be partially reopened, as long as the aforementioned teachers are absent from their work." Before he signed the letter, Karl Aubert added that the school council had unanimously voted to send the letter to the Ministry.[352]

Arnold Bekker was released on May 11, just a few days after the letter was sent, while Lars Dahle was not released until September 9, 1942.[353]

Even though class 1D had not had regular instruction, they were nonetheless given final exams in the written subjects of Norwegian, German, arithmetic, and English in the spring of 1942. Kathe Lasnik received a T- (satisfactory-) in Norwegian, an NG+ (average+) in German, a T (satisfactory) in math, and an NG- (average-) in English.

With those grades, she was number four out of fourteen girls and number seven or eight out of all twenty-three students in class 1D.[354]

Per Wilhelmsen attended classes 1D and 2D with Kathe Lasnik. He later married Fride Prytz, who had lived on the fourth floor of the apartment building on Hertzbergs gate. That was one of the first things I was told by the other classmates. I had talked to Fride Wilhelmsen, naturally, because she supposedly took the farewell letter to school. However, she had not actually done that, because she was hospitalized on November 26, 1942 and knew nothing about the farewell letter at all. Her husband, Per Wilhelmsen, could not remember Mr. Norløff reading a letter from Kathe Lasnik on November 26, 1942.

Jon Andreas Reiersrud, another of the boys from 1D, remembered Kathe Lasnik well. As I understood, he lived alone in a house on Oslo's west side. When I visited him, I brought with me a copy of Norvald Greina's records. Norvald Greina's lessons had not exactly been a pleasure, but when Reiersrud looked at the records, he was shocked. He did not remember getting such poor grades in the first year of junior high. Still, he had eventually shaped up and had graduated from high school in 1946.

Kathe Lasnik, he told me, had not been able to conceal her feelings. When she fell in love with someone, all the boys knew it; however, the boy in question had not returned her feelings. I was extremely interested, of course, and I speculated on who it might have been, but he would not spill the beans. We chatted back and forth a bit. I had Kathe Lasnik's passport pictures with me, and when we looked at them, he said he thought she had been pretty. I said I could make extra copies and send them to him.

I called a little while later. He had gotten the pictures, so I gathered my courage and asked if she had not fallen for Per Wilhelmsen. The girls in class had told me that he had been something of a looker. But no, it had not been him. And just like that, as soon as I asked the question, I knew who it was: Jon Andreas Reiersrud himself. He admitted it right away. Apparently, he had been in a clique with Per Wilhelmsen, Odd Egil Mølstad, and Kari Larsen, so the whole thing was out of the question. However, her crush had quickly passed. After a while, it had been another boy in the class, but he was not interested either.

At this point, I heard how Kathe Lasnik had tried to approach Jon Andreas Reiersrud as he stood on the edge of the façade at Jacob Aalls gate 55, cleaning windows for his mother. She had been walking, had stopped, looked at him, and said: "You're a busy one, aren't you?" Her voice was a little teasing; there were certainly more amusing things to do than clean windows. Jon Andreas Reiersrud had not known quite what to say, and so he had continued with the windows. Kathe Lasnik had stood and watched him for a little while, and then she had left.[355]

19

Elias Lasnik and Leopold Bermann Avoid Arrest

ABOUT THE SAME time that class 2D met again after summer break of 1942, Ambassador Finn Koren from the Norwegian legation in Bern, Switzerland, reported to the Minister of Foreign Affairs, Trygve Lie, in London: "The most gruesome reports are coming out of Poland about the treatment to which the unfortunate Jews are being subjected, and as far as one can tell, it looks like they are trying to 'liquidate' the entire race. The things going on in the Warsaw ghetto simply defy description. About a third of the Jewish population there is already estimated to be dead." Finn Koren also reported about the fate of those Jews deported from the Netherlands: "A large percentage is known with certainty to have already been killed, either by gas, which is probably the most practical and quickest method, or by strychnine. It seems that Hitler believes Jews must be eradicated from the surface of the earth, or at least the European part of it, by any means necessary."[356]

In a coded express telegram, State Police Chief Karl A. Martinsen ordered that all Jewish men over fifteen years of age with a "J" stamp on their passports be arrested at 6:00 a.m. on Monday, October 26, 1942. The State Police, police chiefs, and district sheriffs received a telegram at 10:30 a.m. on Sunday, October 25: The men were to be brought to the Gardekaserne, the royal guard barracks, on Kirkeveien 23, Oslo; their assets were to be seized; their apartments searched for bank notes, jewelry, and cash; their bank accounts closed; and their safety deposit boxes emptied. All adult Jewish women were to be required to report daily to the "patrolmen's criminal division."[357]

Karl A. Martinsen had received orders from Wilhelm Wagner of the German Security Police in Oslo. After the war, Wagner insisted that he himself had received orders from Heinrich Fehlis and Hellmuth Reinhard, who had gotten theirs from Police General Wilhelm Rediess in Oslo, who had received his orders directly from Reinhard Heydrich, or from the Reich's Security Office IV in Berlin.[358]

After the express telegram was sent, all the men from the State Police went to work preparing for the arrests in Oslo and Aker. At 11:30 p.m. on Sunday evening, Inspector Sverre Dürbeck, Inspector Jørgen Wiermyhr, and Assistant Chief of Police Unhjem from the Ministry of the Police arrived at the State Police offices at Henrik Ibsens gate 7 with "Jewish forms" (questionnaires that the Jews themselves filled out). These forms were used to compile names and addresses for "the coming campaign."[359] At the same time, instructions were written out for the patrols and a three-page form, which would be used in the seizing of assets, was stenciled.

Every man from the State Police force was called in, as well as 40 men from the Oslo Criminal Police, everyone enrolled in the State Police Investigation Course, and 20 men from the German SS in Norway. All were supposed to gather together on Monday morning at 5:30 a.m.[360] State Police Chief Karl A. Martinsen instructed those assembled that "wrist watches should be confiscated, since they can be given to soldiers on the front who do not have a watch."[361] There were 52 patrol units,[362] each of which was given a list with ten names and addresses.

Police patrol unit #17, which comprised Officer R. Borgen and Ove Hagen, arrived at Hertzbergs gate 7 to arrest Elias Lasnik.[363] They must have arrived later in the day, because it was Dora Lasnik who signed the confiscation form. Had Anna Lasnik and Elise Lasnik not already gone to the stores, they would have signed the form. Kathe Lasnik might have been at home, since Fagerborg School students had afternoon instruction every other Monday. The apartment, the two stores, a piece of jewelry, and four bankbooks were seized. Dora Lasnik was told to report to Hegdehaugen police station at Schultz' gate 1. At the top of the form, R. Borgen noted that Elias Lasnik was currently in Lovisenberg Hospital. Dora Lasnik wrote her own name on the dotted line for "the prisoner's signature"[364]

At Storgaten 37, patrol unit #9 with Dahlin and Olav Feyling had come to arrest Leopold Bermann,[365] and pounded on the door. The family had moved from Ullevål Hageby to an apartment in the building where he had his dental practice. However, it was only Jenny Bermann and her son who were at home. She explained that her husband "was vacationing someplace in Telemark," but that she expected him home in a week. Though there was not much to seize, police patrol unit #9 did not leave Storgaten 37 completely empty-handed. They closed the dentist's office, seized a wristwatch, took 500 kroner in cash, and learned that the husband had a safety deposit box. Jenny Bermann was told to report to the Møllergaten police station.[366]

Earlier that same day, Julius Bassist placed a call from A. Sangwill A/S, a tailor shop at Lybekkergaten 1, where he worked, to his fiancée at Trondhjemsveien Kitchen Supplies. He told Elise Lasnik to immediately close the store and come to him. He had a Swedish passport and had arranged for a quick wedding at the courthouse. That way Elise Lasnik could also get a Swedish passport and be out of danger. She did what he asked and afterwards the newlyweds went to the restaurant Bagatelle and ate lunch. When Elise Lasnik came home and told her mother that she had gotten married, they opened a can of fish balls.[367] Elise Bassist moved in with Julius Bassist at Gardeveien 2 in Marienlyst, just above the Majorstua subway station.

There had been rumors that a campaign against the Jews was approaching. These rumors were revived on October 22 when a Norwegian border policeman was shot on the train to Halden at Berg Station by a Norwegian man, who was escorting refugees. Nearly every member of the Hermann Gettler family was among the refugees. Since they were sitting at another place on the train, however, they arrived at the prearranged station after the shooting incident, only to stand down by Iddefjorden and wait for a boat that never came. Instead of departing, they were arrested and sent to Halden.[368] On

Saturday, October 24, the front-page headline of the NS newspaper read: "Another Outrageous Death – Norwegian Policeman Gunned Down by Jews."[369]

On Sunday, October 25, Elias Lasnik was admitted for his chronic illness to Room 151 in the medical division at Diakonissehusets Hospital (now Lovisenberg Hospital) by Dr. Storm Herseth. Chief Physician Otto Jervell then took charge of Elias Lasnik, who at the time of his admittance weighed only 51 kg.[370]

The day before police patrol unit #9 had pounded on the door of their apartment at Storgaten 37, Leopold Bermann had crossed the Swedish border at Dalen in Töcksmark parish. He told Swedish authorities that he had two brothers and two brothers-in-law who had been arrested, and that on Friday, October 23, he had received a telephone call from a friend warning him that his arrest was imminent. On Saturday morning, October 24, he had taken the train from Oslo to Mysen, and from there he had made his way alone to the border and on the morning of October 25 had crossed into Sweden,[371] where he was captured by a Swedish border patrol.[372]

The refugee was handed over to Åke Hiertner, a District Attorney in Koppom in the district of Järnskog. Hiertner then asked the Ministry of Foreign Affairs' Passport Office for instructions about what to do with the Norwegian. The Ministry decided that Leopold Bermann would be given an "emergency visa" for the time period between October 25 and November 7, 1942. On Monday, October 26, he was sent to a reception center for Norwegian refugees at Kjesäter camp. Leopold Bermann arrived at the camp on October 27 and was given refugee number 9,811. Three days later he was sent to Öreryd, a refugee camp in Småland.[373]

In total, 258 male Jews were arrested in Oslo and Aker on October 26. There were only 90 arrested that same day in the rest of the country and all of these were eventually sent to the Berg concentration camp at Tønsberg.[374]

20

Supreme Court Lawyer Mellbye Protests

AFTER THE WAR, Inspector Knut Rød, head of the State Police's Oslo and Aker divisions, explained that he had received orders from Karl A. Martinsen to make what he called "the technical arrangements" for the arrest of the Jewish men. He "had not actually" expected these orders, but he "was not terribly surprised either," given the series of "anti-Semitic articles in the press" during the fall.[375] According to the report issued by the State Police regarding the arrests, Inspector Rød had worked "nonstop from Sunday 10:00 a.m. until Monday 10:00 p.m."[376]

Knut Rød was born in Kristiania in 1900 and received his law degree in 1927. That same year he was hired as an officer in the Aker police department under Chief Johan Søhr, who had strongly cautioned against admitting Jews into the country during World War I and who had spoken out against the Jewish method of slaughtering animals in 1927. In 1929, Knut Rød became an inspector and in 1937 a police lieutenant in Aker's criminal division. When the police divisions in Oslo and Aker were combined in the fall of 1940, Knut Rød was transferred to the Surveillance Division. He joined the NS on January 4, 1941. When the State Police department was established, Knut Rød became the administrative head of the Oslo division. He quit the State Police department on September 15, 1943 and left the NS on September 30, 1943.[377]

The National Archives in Stockholm holds the reports that the Swedish legation in Oslo sent to the Ministry of Foreign Affairs. Claes Westring of the Swedish Consulate General had already written on Thursday, October 27, to Staffan Söderblom in the Ministry of Foreign Affairs about the raid on the Norwegian Jews. He dismissed outright the idea that these arrests were a reprisal for the killing of a Norwegian policeman on the Halden train: "The raid would have happened sooner or later even without that incident." He also pointed out that a number of Jews had already been arrested during the martial law period in Trondhjem, which lasted from October 6 through 10, 1942.[378]

The Swedish Consulate General also touched on what the Norwegian press was saying about the raid. In the Nazified press, the arrests were being represented as "a reaction against the Jews' positively hostile attitude toward to the new Norwegian state, an attitude connected with Jewish Bolshevism and the Jewish high financial powers' bitter fight against national movements the world over." On October 26, furthermore, Claes Westring had visited the head of the German Security Police, Heinrich Fehlis, because a Swedish Jew had also been arrested. Fehlis answered that their intention was not to arrest Jews with Swedish citizenship, but that he hoped that they would go back to Sweden as soon as possible.[379]

The Swedish Consulate General, however, could not report any widespread opposition to the persecution of Jews in Oslo. Still, there were some protests. Just after October 26, Supreme Court lawyer Mellbye had gone to the Norwegian State Police and protested against the seizure of "all Jewish assets." What were the [Jewish] women and children supposed to live on after their providers had been arrested and their sources of revenue seized? The State Police had answered that in that case they could do what they did in Germany: the rich Jews would help the poor. But in Germany, Mellbye pointed out, not all the grown men had been arrested as they had been in Norway. Here there was no one left to look after the women and children. The State Police then suggested that Mellbye go to the Jews, but the Supreme Court lawyer said that he did not know any Jews. The result of Mellbye's protest was that the chairman of the Jewish Aid Committee was released, and he began to organize assistance.[380]

During the fall of 1942, the Swedish Ministry of Foreign Affairs had received a number of reports from various sources regarding factory-like extermination camps in Poland. The Swedish Consulate General in Stettin had reported as early as August 20, 1942, that mass murders were being carried out in Poland and that gas was being used.[381] Added to this, another Swede, diplomat Göran von Otter, who was connected with the Swedish Embassy in Berlin, is supposed to have reported a meeting with SS Lieutenant Kurt Gerstein. They apparently met one another on a train between Warsaw and Berlin on August 22, 1942. Gerstein had taken part in the gassings at the concentration camp of Belzec, and wanted to make the mass murders known to the world. During a conversation that lasted several hours, Gerstein told von Otter everything he knew. According to von Otter's report: "After a near collapse that the man only overcame with great difficulty, he said that he was returning from an excursion he had been sent on to visit a corpse factory in Belzec, which is a little east of Lublin. After that, he described the gassing process and gave me all the details that I asked for, so I could check the accuracy of his information regarding transportation, technical processes, victims, the reactions of supervisory SS personnel and hands-on Ukrainian workers, the treatment of the victims before and after execution, the seizure of jewelry, gold teeth, hidden valuables, the burial procedure, and so on. I was shown documents, orders for cyanide, identity cards, and so on."[382] Some people believe that the source of the report is questionable, because there is no memo dating from August 1942 regarding von Otter in the Swedish Ministry of Foreign Affairs, but only one from July 1945.[383]

However, when Gösta Engzell, who was Swedish Secretary General during the war, was questioned about the matter in 1970, he said that the details provided by von Otter were the first "direct information" about what was happening in the Polish camps. The Swedish historian Paul A. Levine interprets this to mean that Gösta Engzell had already received less trustworthy information about what was happening in Poland, and that these reports had reached Sweden in the fall of 1942.

On September 7, 1942, Gösta Engzell of the Ministry of Foreign Affairs visited the Jewish businessman Gillel Storch. Storch was from Riga, but was living as a refugee in Stockholm. He confidentially told Engzell that he had been in contact with relatives in Lettland, who had described the "unheard-of horrors and suffering" that Jews were experiencing.[384] Gösta Engzell drafted a memo after his meeting with Gillel Storch, which was shared with Christian Günther, the Minister of Foreign Affairs.[385]

Before Norway carried out the arrests of the Jewish men, both the Swedish Ministry of Foreign Affairs and the Norwegian Minister of Foreign Affairs, Trygve Lie, had received more or less the same information about what was happening in the Polish concentration camps. Paul A. Levine argues that Engzell believed this information.[386] No one knows what Trygve Lie thought. In any case, he did nothing. What could the Swedes do?

21

Keeping Silent Means Being Accountable

IN ARRESTING JEWISH men and ordering Jewish women to report to local police stations, the State Police made it difficult for many women to immigrate to Sweden. Not many women wanted to leave their husbands once they had been arrested. In addition, women had fewer contacts than men; perhaps they did not even know anyone that they could ask to help get them out of the country. The same was true of families whose men had gone to Sweden.

Every day Dora Lasnik reported to the police station at Schultz' gate 1, while Jenny Bermann reported to the police station at Møller-gaten 19.

Celia Century fled the country together with her family at 1:00 p.m. on November 4 and traveled by car from Oslo to Grue. At 11:30 p.m. they crossed the border and were immediately arrested by a Swedish military patrol, who then handed them over to the local prosecutor at 8:30 a.m. the next morning. From there they were sent to Kjesäter.[387] Celia Century's father had gone into hiding when the men were arrested, and he fled the country with his family.

On November 7, Inger-Johanne Berg stood with her mother in their apartment on the third floor at Hertzbergs gate 7B and observed Elise and Julius Bassist leaving. The mother said to her daughter: "Something is going to happen very soon now."[388] With their Swedish passports, Julius and Elise Bassist could legally travel to Sweden, and they had begun making plans the moment they were married. She had tried to add Jenny Bermann's small son to her own passport, but it did not work. The newlyweds had packed some suitcases and sent them ahead, and on Sunday, November 7 they traveled with the rest of their luggage by train from Østbanen in Oslo to Stockholm. The customs at Kongsvinger Station took two hours. A German soldier pointed to the "J" on Elise Bassist's identification papers and said: "You won't be needing that in Sweden!"[389]

Norwegian church leaders, with Professor Hellesby from the Norwegian School of Theology at their head, protested the persecution of the Jews in a long letter addressed to Minister-President Vidkun Quisling, dated November 11, 1942. It was the arrests, not to mention the law permitting the seizure of Jewish assets, that had upset the church leaders. "For 91 years Jews had a legal right to settle and provide for themselves in our country. Now, however, they are being stripped of their possessions without warning and afterward the men are being arrested, preventing them from providing for their propertyless wives and children. This is contrary to not only the Christian teaching concerning neighborly love, but also the most basic claim to civil rights. These Jews have not been accused, much less convicted, of breaking any of the country's laws. And nonetheless they are being punished as severely as the worst of criminals. They are being punished for their heritage, for the simple fact that they are Jews."

The letter further argued that the "government's rejection of the human dignity of the Jews" was directly opposed to God's word, which "from cover to cover maintains that all people are of one blood." In God's eyes, all people have "the same basic human dignity and therefore the same human rights." The church leaders also asserted that they found themselves "in the deepest distress. [...] By remaining silent in the face of this legalized injustice against the Jews, we become answerable for and complicit in that injustice. [...] Halt the persecution of the Jews and stop the racial hatred that is being spread by the press in our country."[390]

Elias Lasnik was given a thorough examination at Lovisenberg Hospital. He tried to stand up for a while, but was forced to lie down again. During the night, his cough deprived him of sleep, his appetite was poor, and he did not gain weight.[391]

The doctor for the State Police, Dr. Hans Eng, drafted a form[392] to be filled out for every Jew who was admitted to the hospital after October 26. Chief Physician Otto Jervell filled out the form for Elias Lasnik on November 10. Besides requiring the diagnosis and the "most significant symptoms and objective findings,"[393] the form also asked when the illness had broken out, if there was a need for treatment, and if a doctor's supervision was actually necessary. Finally, the State Police doctor wanted to know how long it would take before the patient was well again. Because Elias Lasnik had a chronic illness, however, Jervell could give no definite answer. He also answered in the negative to Dr. Eng's last question, namely, whether "aggravation or simulation" was present.

Dr. Otto Jervell stamped and returned the form to the State Police. Dr. Eng looked the form over, decided that the patient "could be collected," and on November 17 State Policeman Gustav Ruud traveled to Lovisenberg Hospital to arrest Elias Lasnik. Afterward, he reported that: "I tried to arrest the Jew Elias Lasnik, who was lying sick at Lovisenberg Hospital, but Chief Physician Jervell would not release him from the hospital. He insisted it was dangerous for his illness." Next to Dr. Hans Eng's "can be collected," Dr. Otto Jervell had written: "Staying here."[394]

The same day that the State Police had tried to arrest Elias Lasnik at the hospital, the Møllergaten police department reported that Jenny Bermann "had not checked in." Constable R. A. Hansen of the Oslo and Aker division conferred with Detective Homb, who asked the constable to go down to Storgaten 37. He rang the bell multiple times, but finally had to call the porter. As R. A. Hansen reports, "upon inspection here [I] found that the furniture was still in place, but the woman's closet was empty. I consider it likely that the woman has left."[395] The next day, State Police Sergeant F. Myrvold reported that "the guard at the Patrol Section" had not yet confirmed that Jenny Bermann had checked in.[396]

There was a good reason for that. On Sunday, November 15, Jenny Bermann and her son were helped across the border at Töckmark parish in Sweden.[397] When she was questioned by the assistant local prosecutor there, she explained that she was of Jewish descent and was married to the dentist Leopold Bermann, who had fled to Sweden on October 25. She wanted to join her husband. Furthermore, the reason for her flight "was the persecution of Jews in Norway that was taking place." Jenny Bermann and her son were then given an "emergency visa," and on November 17 they traveled to Kjesäter, where they received refugee numbers 10,471 and 10,472. After spending two days in the refugee camp, they were able to travel to Stockholm.[398]

22

Kathe Lasnik Fills Out Her Questionnaire

IN MID-NOVEMBER, 1942, Kathe Lasnik was living with both her mother and her sister, Anna Lasnik, at Hertzbergs gate 7. Her father was hospitalized in Lovisenberg. Her other two sisters, their husbands, and her little nephew were in Sweden; or rather, Jenny Bermann and her son were on their way to Sweden. It must have felt strange to have so few people in the apartment. After all, Kathe Lasnik had been used to beds in every room that were filled with adults who breathed and slept and turned during the night.

November in Oslo is the darkest month of the year. With December comes white snow that brightens everything up, even if it only lasts for a few days. On Monday, November 16, 1942, the sun rose at 8:16 a.m. and set at 3:47 p.m. The day was twelve hours and forty-nine minutes shorter than at the summer solstice.

Since class 2D had afternoon instruction, the students walked home through a dark city with carbide lights. They were often stopped and asked to show identification. The girls in 2D were longing to be bicycled home by Steinar Steinarsson from Harald Hårfagres gate 12.[399] Kathe Lasnik, too, dreamed about getting to sit on the luggage rack on the back of his bike. Unfortunately for these girls, he had his eye on Aud Holmsen of Kirkeveien 74. School had been held in private homes during the fuel crisis vacation that took place in the spring of 1942, and the students had sat so close together that it was easy to fall in love.[400]

On November 16, Dora Lasnik went to the police station at Schultz' gate 1 to fulfill her obligation to report. At that time, she probably delivered the "Questionnaire for the Jews in Norway," which Kathe Lasnik had just completed. Presumably, Kathe's mother had been given the form a few days before and told that her daughter, who was now 15, was required to fill it out.

The "Questionnaire for Jews in Norway," which was five pages long, had to be filled out in triplicate. A typewriter was preferable. Dotted lines showed where the answers to the questions were to be written. "Last Name" was the first piece of information for which it asked, and small letters added: "For women also maiden name." She wrote "Lasnik." After that: "Full first name," and in small letters: "Name used should be underlined." She wrote "Kathe Rita," and underlined Kathe.

For "Born (place, date, year)," she answered in the opposite order with "13/10-27 Oslo"; "In what country" with "Norway"; and "Home addr. (st. nr., city)" with "Hertzbergs gt 7B Oslo." She left "Home tel." blank and did not write "82 342." "Present religious community": "mosaic"; and for the question, "For how long," she wrote "since birth."

In answer to "Family status: (Unmarried, married, widow, divorced)" she wrote "Unmarried." That was the correct answer, of course. However, her official civil status was not actually "unmarried," but rather "child in a family." Kathe Lasnik drew a long blue line across the dotted lines for the questions: "First and last name of spouse"; "Spouse's birthplace, date, and year"; and "Number of children."

After "Present occupation," she wrote "School student." After that, she went back and crossed out the "yes" she had previously written in answer to the question about whether her present occupation was "Independent." She also put pen to paper and crossed out everything pertaining to occupation by trade, secondary profession, military education, public office, and membership in professional organizations.

"Have you been a Freemason?" Kathe Lasnik wrote, "No." "Nationality": "Norwegian." "Citizenship": "Norwegian." And to the question: "When did you come to Norway," she wrote "I've always been in Norway." She could have skipped over that last one, but she did not. Presumably, she thought it would help her.

Kathe Lasnik proceeded to cross out the entire next page, which asked questions regarding any businesses. When she got to the question about assets and real estate, however, she answered, "nothing." She also crossed out the third page, which again asked questions about businesses. To the last question on the form, which asked if she had ever been reported, charged with a crime, fined or sentenced, she answered "No."

Finally, she wrote: "Oslo 16/11-42" and signed her name "K. Lasnik."

The form would be sent to the Oslo Police Presidium, where on November 21, Detective Inspector A. Berg verified that, indeed, Kathe Lasnik had never been charged with a crime, punished or fined.[401]

23

Real Estate Owners Raise Their Voices

THE KITCHEN SUPPLY shops on Markveien and Trondhjemsveien were seized by the Liquidation Board for Confiscated Jewish Property. The office was established immediately after the Act relating to the Confiscation of Jewish Assets was signed by Minister-President Vidkun Quisling on October 26, 1942.[402]

Haakon Høst, a lawyer, was declared trustee for all property seized from Elias Lasnik, which consisted of the two shops and the apartment on Hertzbergs gate.[403] Høst was born in 1905 to two Norwegian parents and was baptized and confirmed in Oslo. He graduated from Oslo Cathedral School in 1924 and received his law degree in 1933. After taking his exams, he worked as a proxy for Supreme Court lawyer Eivind Saxlund, who authored the anti-Semitic book *Jews and Goyim*, published in 1910. After Saxlund's death, Høst opened his own legal practice in 1937.[404] Haakon Høst joined the NS in October, 1940.

In the statement he gave after the war, Høst maintained that he was "ignorant of the treatment to which the Jews were being subjected" and that the "deportation" of the Jews had been a "German affair."[405] After the war, Haakon Høst was also quite vocal about the fact that the Liquidation Board had had "a lot of trouble with the Germans during its operations."[406] Apparently, the Germans often tended to show up and help themselves to seized Jewish property before representatives from the Liquidation Board arrived. Haakon Høst, however, did not want to have anything to do with that. Instead, he maintained that the

Liquidation Board had, in fact, "protected Norwegian interests" and had done "a good job."[407]

The Liquidation Board published lists of seized properties at the beginning of November in both the public annoucements, *Offentlige Kunngjøringer*, and the NS's own newspaper, *Fritt Folk*. Anyone who had a claim on these properties was instructed to contact the office within the month. The first to speak up regarding Elias Lasnik's seized assets was the landlord for Markveien 58. Ingvar Nielsen had a number of things he wanted to address, as he informed lawyer Haakon Høst on November 18, 1942. In the first place, the rent for Markveien Kitchen Supplies had been paid in advance. Since it had only been paid through November 1, however, who would pay the 202.50 kroner that Anna Lasnik owed for the month of November? According to the contract's termination clause, there was also a two-month termination fee. Who would pay that? Furthermore, the plate glass window that faced Markveien had cracked in one corner when Elias Lasnik had installed wooden boards to protect against bombings. Now that the landlord was finally going to install a new window pane, could he send the bill to the Liquidation Board? Furthermore, the building's water and sewer pipes ran through the store's back room. When the cold set in and the room had to be heated so the pipes would not freeze, who would pay for the heating? To the landlord's thinking, all these costs should obviously be charged against Elias Lasnik's property.[408]

Could the landlord not have asked Anna Lasnik about it? She was home at Hertzbergs gate 7B and had been a tenant at Markveien 58 since 1934. According to the rental records, she had always paid punctually.[409] By approaching Haakon Høst with these financial claims, the landlord was essentially treating his tenant, Anna Lasnik, as a nonexistent person, at least in legal terms.

The owner of Heimdalsgate 2 was also quick to make contact. D. V. Sundsten wanted to know what he should do about the two "Jewish shop tenants in my building," who had "had to close their businesses." The barber Zakken Hurwitz owed 50.50 kroner for the

November rent. However, the only things of value in the shop were two old barber chairs, which were not worth enough to cover that sum. Elise Bassist's kitchen supply store did not fare much better. The shelves were almost empty; all that was left were "impractical objects" that altogether would probably "fit into a good-sized wheelbarrow." At any rate, he did not think their combined value would cover the rent for November, which amounted to 135.75 kroner. The landlord, furthermore, had taken it upon himself to store the goods for free until they could be sold, so that he could at least rent out the spaces.[410]

How in the world could D. V. Sundsten claim that on November 24 there were not enough goods on the shelves in Trondhjemsveien Kitchen Supplies to cover November's rent? According to an undated Liquidation Board inventory list, which was made out by lawyer Haakon Høst, manager Knut Haagensen, and K. Berg, Elise Lasnik's shop contained goods worth 5,274.60 kr.[411] As it turns out, however, the Liquidation Board had sold all that inventory before November 24! Johs. Leborg of the firm Johs. Leborg and Co. had actually picked everything up before the landlord even wrote to the Liquidation Board. Johs. Leborg had bid 2,892.28 kroner on the contents of Elise Lasnik's shop. "I think it is a good offer," Haakon Høst opined, further pointing out that Johs. Leborg was an NS member.[412] Johs. Leborg also bought the inventory of Markveien Kitchen Supplies.

A number of firms also made claims. A/S Stormbull, which had stocks and securities totaling a dizzying 2,000,000 kr., sent a bill to tinsmith Elias Lasnik, who just before he was hospitalized had picked up 26 kilos of round steel bars and 23 kilos of black steel band "5/8 x 1/8" for a total of 29.14 kr.[413] These supplies were for a wartime project Elias Lasnik had begun, which involved installing trash containers in a small workshop on Hausmanns gate.[414]

Kaare O. Wiken A/S, the Oslo municipal tax collector; Chr.a. Glass Warehouse; K. E. Larsson A/S; Lilleborg Manufacturers; Halvorsen & Larsen A/S; Rolf Brynhildsen; Oslo Electric; Oslo's Social Security Office; Ødegaard Brothers – all made their claims. Germaneren, the Action Committee for the German SS Norway, sent a bill for the installation of a new dressing room shelf at Hertzbergs gate 7; A/S Rafens Eftf. and Kosmetica A/S also made claims on the estate of Elias Lasnik.[415] Indeed, it seemed that no one had any qualms about letting their demands be known.

On the day that the landlord of Heimdalsgaten 2 addressed his concerned letter to lawyer Haakon Høst at the Liquidation Board, *Aftenposten* published an article with the headline: "Martin Luther's Opinion on Jews: Stop Their Usury and Take from Them All the Money and Property They Have Stolen from Us." Apparently, *Aftenposten* had gotten hold of volume 23 of the scholarly Erlander edition of Luther's collected works: "Burn their synagogues and schools, and what does not burn up should be covered with earth so that no Christian will ever see the stones and cinders again. [...] Destroy their houses for the same reason. They do there what they do in the synagogues. Let them live in sheds and stalls like gypsies, so that they will learn that they are not the masters of our land, as they [have] proclaimed. [...] Prohibit Jews from using our streets. They have no business there. Let them stay at home. If their usury is not stopped, an army might someday need to be assembled against them, [simply] because they were not forbidden to show themselves in the streets and no steps were taken to ward off their practices."[416]

24

A Hospital Arrest

ON THURSDAY, NOVEMBER 24, at 10:00 p.m., Karl A. Martinsen, the State Police chief, received a "notification," as he put it in a report he wrote three days later, from Hauptsturmführer Wagner – namely, that everyone with a "J" stamp was to be evacuated from Norway. "A ship for this purpose will be available to depart from Oslo on Thursday, November 26, 1942 ca. 3:00 p.m."[417] A few hours later, the head of the secret German State Police in Norway, the Gestapo, SS Stürmbannführer Hellmuth Reinhard, informed his colleagues in Stettin that a ship would leave from Oslo on November 26 carrying somewhere between 700 and 900 female and male Jews of every age. He estimated that the voyage would last three days. Therefore, the Gestapo in Stettin should ensure that further transport was available, because the *Donau* must immediately set out to sea again. "The Jews should be taken to Auschwitz,"[418] Reinhard clarified at the end of his message.

At the same time, it was probably due to the short deadline given the Norwegian State Police force that it was not actually clear until November 24 that the troop transport ship, *Donau* – set to arrive in Oslo with convalescents from General Paulus's sixth army division in Stalingrad[419] – had no return cargo when it was ready to sail from Oslo to Stettin on November 26.

On the morning of November 26, the Assistant Chief of Police, Knut Rød, was called in by Karl A. Martinsen and told to coordinate the arrest of everyone with a passport and ID marked with a "J."[420] As Karl A. Martinsen wrote: "What required the most work and was most difficult to execute" was the planning and "detention of the Jewish families (women and children) in the Oslo police district."[421] This task fell to Assistant Chief Knut Rød. As early as November 25, the men in his division had had their hands full drawing up lists of those to "be detained." One hundred patrol teams were then assembled, each consisting of "a policeman, who would act as patrol leader, + two helpers (NS or SS men or policemen). Every patrol [will have] a taxi put at his disposal."

Every patrol leader, furthermore, was given four lists or addresses. The arrests were organized in the following way: Patrol leader gave one list to "helper" number one and one list to "helper" number two, at which point the helpers would go to each address and detain the family. In the meantime, the patrol leader would take list number three, go to the address, arrest the family and deliver them to Pier 1, where the arrested family would be transferred. The truck would then drive back to helper number one, "load the family into the car, and drive to Pier nr. 1, at the same time as list number 4 is given to helper number one, who would then go as quickly as possible to the address on the list, in order to detain and get the family ready."[422]

Preparations for the Jewish arrests continued more or less unbroken through Wednesday and into Thursday. However, on Wednesday, November 25, at 10:00 p.m., even more work was created for the Norwegian State Police when the Germans discovered that the rules governing the arrests needed to be changed: namely, "it had now been decided that families with one Aryan spouse should not be evacuated at all." Regarding this mandatory change, Karl A. Martinsen wrote in his report that: "It caused us a considerable headache, since the process was already well under way, according to the original guidelines."[423] It was this change that saved Moritz Gorvitz, since he was married to a non-Jewish Norwegian woman.

Knut Rød requisitioned an additional "60 officers from the Oslo Criminal Police, ca. 100 from Support Division, 60 NS men and 30 SS men from German SS Norway." Three hundred men and 100 taxis were to meet up at Kirkeveien 23 on November 26 at 4:30 a.m. "for instructions."[424]

On Wednesday evening, the State Police in Oslo had already headed out to arrest people with a "J" stamp who were in "hospitals and other institutions." These people would be brought to Bredtvedt Prison, where they would remain "until loading could begin."[425] Inspector Ragnvald Kranz had at first been given the task, but he "immediately realized that arresting the old and infirm would be a horrible job." Therefore, he arranged to be in Berg at the time, organizing the transport of the interned men from Tønsberg to Oslo, and so instructed Inspector Vogth "to arrest the infirm and old."[426]

When the State Police arrived at Lovisenberg Hospital, Chief Physician Otto Jervell again protested the arrest of his patient. He then documented the proceedings in his journal: "Although it is been made clear that Elias Lasnik, b. 24.12.[18]87 in Lithuania, requires continued hospitalization for a lung infection that could well be contagious, and in any case should be treated with a full hospital regimen, the demand was made that the patient be handed over to the State Police."[427]

Kathe Lasnik was visiting her father when a State Police officer showed up to arrest him. After the officer drove away with Elias Lasnik, furthermore, she went straight to Edith Gjeruldsen and told her exactly what had happened at the hospital. She said that she had clung to her father's arm and tried to hold him back, but the policeman had grabbed her father's other arm and pulled, and that the policeman had proved stronger and that she had finally had to let go.

The girls had sat in Edith Gjeruldsen's room on the second floor of Hertzbergs gate 2 and talked about it. Why had her father been arrested? Where were they taking him? They had decided that he was simply going to be interned together with the other Jewish men until the war was over. Kathe Lasnik had been somewhat reassured by this idea, though not entirely, because when she had crossed the street and headed home to bed on the evening of November 25, 1942, she had left behind the warm jacket that she had been wearing.[428]

25

A Humane Arrest

STATE POLICE CHIEF Karl A. Martinsen was supposed to muster the troops at 4:30 a.m. on Thursday, November 26, before the patrol teams headed out. However, he failed to appear. Therefore, Knut Rød gave orders to the assembled force. After the war, Knut Rød's defense attorney argued that there had been "no way out" for Rød, "since several hundred Norwegian officers were deployed, and a number of Germans were present." As a result, Supreme Court lawyer Leif S. Rode concluded in a letter to the police's Department of Collaborators on September 28, 1945: "A nullification of the endeavor [that Rød had to give orders to the troops] would not be tolerated." Nonetheless, according to his defense attorney, Knut Rød "emphasized" that "the arrests should be carried out humanely and that the Jews should be given time to eat and pack some clothes."[429]

The Supreme Court lawyer did not bother to question how the arrest of children could be called "humane." The Norwegian police had never arrested children before, either in war or in peacetime. As a result, when he defended his actions in the State Police department, Assistant Chief Knut Rød was never forced to acknowledge that the arrests had included children. Instead, he claimed he was just going about "pure police business when he organized the arrests of the Jews."[430] In his written explanation on September 16, 1945, furthermore, Knut Rød maintained that a few days before November 26, Karl A. Martinsen had "told [him]" that the Germans had decided that "Jews, men and women" would be sent to Germany and that they would be gathered together in "colonies in Poland or East Prussia."

After that, he received "orders to arrange the arrest of Jewish women who lived in Oslo and to requisition people from Oslo kripo [Criminal Police] to help."[431]

No doubt Knut Rød intuited that it was ridiculous to talk about "pure police business" when it came to the arrest of children. Therefore, he did not record that he had gotten the order to arrest women and children. In the same way, Supreme Court lawyer Leif S. Rode wrote about the humane arrest of "the Jews."

In addition, the telegram from the Gestapo in Berlin to the Gestapo in Oslo, who ordered the arrests on November 26, 1942, failed to specify that children should be arrested. It only said that the separation of spouses and children under the age of 14 "should be avoided."[432] In fact, no one gave an order stating that children should be arrested; at the same time, no one could have doubted that this was exactly what would occur.

Regarding the arrests of Jewish women and children that took place on the morning of November 26, neither the lists of police patrol units nor the signed seizure forms are available. As a result, the names of the policemen who left the guard barracks at Kirkeveien 23 vis-à-vis the entrance to Vigeland's Sculpture Park and on to Hertzbergs gate 7 are not known. Perhaps Hertzbergs gate 7 was the first stop for the patrol unit, who let off a policeman with orders to arrest Dora Lasnik, Anna Lasnik and Kathe Lasnik.

That policeman must have rung the doorbell, come inside, instructed them to pack enough warm clothing and food for five days, and then remained in the apartment to keep watch until the cab returned to drive them to Pier 1. While she was packing, Kathe Lasnik realized that she did not have her warm jacket, and that, furthermore, she had nothing to use as a suitcase. As a result, she must have asked the policeman if she could go to her friend's house across the street to get her jacket and ask if she could borrow a suitcase.

When the Gjeruldsen family's doorbell rang, it was so early that the first thought to go through her friend's mind when she woke up and heard what the matter concerned, was: could a piece of clothing really be so important in the middle of the night? A policeman stood in the stairway entrance behind Kathe Lasnik, but it was not anyone from the NS or the SS who had come to Hertzbergs gate. It was a regular policeman from the State Police or the Criminal Police.

That policeman kept standing behind Kathe Lasnik, while Edith Gjeruldsen fetched the warm jacket she had forgotten. Edith Gjeruldsen's father also retrieved a canvas suitcase from the attic for her to borrow. When Kathe Lasnik had gotten the suitcase and the jacket, she went home with the policeman.[433]

It was presumably right after Kathe Lasnik went to the Gjeruldsens that she went up to the apartment on the fourth floor of her building and rang the bell. However, it would not have been to say good-bye to Fride Prytz, because Kathe Lasnik knew she was in the hospital. It was probably to say good-bye to Inger Prytz or Birgitte Prytz. Since they were not awake, Kathe Lasnik only saw their mother.[434] According to what Elise Bassist heard after the war, the policeman had asked if there was not someone to whom Kathe Lasnik wanted to say good-bye. Supposedly, this was to give her the chance to escape. In that case, why did he not let her go alone to the Gjeruldsens? Why did he not follow Edith Gjeruldsen's father up to the attic to ask him to hide Kathe Lasnik? There is little evidence that the policeman who came to Hertzbergs gate 7 tried to help anyone escape. Instead, he probably kept a close watch when Kathe Lasnik went up to the fourth floor and rang the Prytz's bell.

Later, the Gjeruldsen family watched from their apartment on the second floor of Hertzbergs gate 2 as Dora Lasnik, Anna Lasnik and Kathe Lasnik were driven away in a low, black car that came from Suhms gate and disappeared up Hertzbergs gate.[435] At Hertzbergs gate 7, Inger-Johanne Berg and her mother stood at their kitchen window and watched as the three were helped into a truck with a high frame and were driven away with their suitcases and bundles. It was light enough by then that they could see the cab down there on the street. It had come from Suhms gate and it disappeared up Hertzbergs gate.[436]

There was perhaps one other person who witnessed the arrest. When lawyer Haakon Høst from the Liquidation Board arrived with two appraisers in order to register the contents of the Lasnik family's apartment on December 2, 1942, they met Miss Mary Bertelsen, who was subletting the maid's room.[437] Dora Lasnik and Anna Lasnik had probably decided to rent out a room. Despite everything, they had not given up. Instead, they had tried to find a way to support themselves.

26

Fagerborg School, November 26

COULD IT HAVE been Mary Bertelsen who gave the farewell letter, if indeed it existed, to class 2D, so that Hans Kristian Norløff could then read it out loud during first period on November 26? Mary Bertelsen, who could not be located, was perhaps the closest eye-witness to the arrest.

Would Kathe Lasnik have indeed tried to escape, had the opportunity presented itself? No, in fact it would probably have taken physical force to separate her from her mother and sister. They were all that she had left, since her father had been arrested the previous evening.

However, it was not only a couple of the girls from the class who remembered Kathe Lasnik's farewell letter. Steinar Steinarsson also thought that something had been read aloud, or that in any case something had been said about the arrests when Kathe Lasnik did not show up for school.[438] Two of the girls even remembered how the letter looked. Apparently, it was only one page long, and she had written it in red crayon.[439] "Thanks for everything. You won't see me again. Last night we were arrested."

Memory can be compared to a hollow sphere. Inside it, experiences, like particles of varying sizes, stir. When they hit the sphere's walls, they vanish, leaving behind traces. Memory is formed by the traces left by the particles on the sphere's walls. However, the sphere is constantly being filled with new particles that leave behind new traces. Though these traces change the character of the original ones, it does not mean that the original memories are lost. Furthermore, within the memory sphere, traces left behind on the wall attract particles of a similar nature. The memory of Kathe Lasnik's deportation and murder are drawn to the smaller traces that Kathe Lasnik left behind earlier, creating with their collision a crater large enough to destroy almost everything that went before it. Although a few small traces still survive around it, they are almost impossible to recover.

Those who knew Kathe Lasnik want to talk almost exclusively about the arrest: how she clung to her father's arm in the hospital to stop the policeman from taking him away; the policeman who took her across the street so that she could get her warm jacket and borrow a suitcase, and who asked her if she had anyone to whom she wanted to bid farewell. Was it perhaps after she went up to the fourth floor and did not see her friends that she decided to write the farewell letter?

One of the girls claimed that Elias Lasnik's arrest had taken place at Hertzbergsgate. Kathe Lasnik supposedly fought with the policeman, while the whole street looked on, hands hanging helpless at their sides. I know that this was not the case. The struggle took place in Room 151 at Lovisenberg Hospital.

Kathe Lasnik, indignant that her ID papers had been stamped with a "J," went over to a friend's apartment. She had been undaunted by the fact that the man who had come to arrest her father wore a police uniform. She had clung to her father's arm nonetheless. The next morning, when the vehicle came from Suhms gate, drove up Hertzbergsgate, and stopped outside of 7B, the street was completely deserted.

According to *Meldungen aus Norwegen*, or *News from Norway*, a classified newsletter belonging to the German Security Police, rumors about the arrest spread "like wildfire among the population, though without arousing any extraordinary interest."[440]

In the attendance record for class 2D, Norvald Greina marked Kathe Lasnik absent for three days in October, and it appears that she would have received a T (satisfactory) on her first report card after the summer vacation. He did not bother to mark her absent for November, probably because she had already been taken away. In the grade column for October and November, Greina drew a short, straight line, and put a small question mark next to her name. These are the only visible traces Kathe Lasnik's arrest left in the school's archives.

Another girl from Fagerborg School, Rachel Feinberg, was also arrested on November 26.[441] When Lars Dahle and Arnold Bekker, both teachers at Fagerborg School, were arrested, Principal Karl Aubert wrote a letter of protest demanding their release, an act, moreover, that received unanimous support from the school council on May 7, 1942. Indeed, before the letter was sent to the Ministry of Church Affairs and Education, it directly quoted the council: "The arrest of these teachers has horrified not only teachers, but also students and their parents."[442] When Kathe Lasnik and Rachel Feinberg were arrested six months later, however, no new letter from the principal that had first been drafted by the school council was unanimously submitted to the Ministry. Furthermore, no other school is known to have sent communiqués demanding to know what happened to all the arrested students.[443] In Oslo, a total of 23 school-aged children were arrested,[444] that is, a couple of students from every school.

But Kathe Lasnik's friend, Inger Becker, was helped by Mr. Petersen, a teacher at Sinsen High School. He had said: "If anything happens to [your family], come to me, no matter if it is day or night."[445] I wanted to find out what I could about this teacher. However, when I rang the doorbell of Inger Becker's apartment, which was located in Västra Skogen, a young woman answered. She told me that Inger Becker had passed away.

Her right arm had been hurting the last time I had visited her and she had been to see a doctor numerous times. However, he had been unable to discover what was wrong with her. Despite that, in April 2001 she had been in good spirits and, as she had done for years, had continued her work as a tour guide in Stockholm throughout the spring and summer. After graduating from the Norwegian High School in Uppsala in June 1945, she had studied at the Sorbonne for a while, and had received an MA from Stockholm University. After 1962, she had worked for the National Labor Market Board in

Stockholm. She had also written articles for *Dagens Nyheter*, or the *Daily News*, and in 1977 had published a novel, *To Be or Not to Be*. During the spring of 2001, she had been worried about whether or not she would still be able to give tours. She was 75 years old and only a substitute. Still, the previous summer had been busy enough. She had preferred Norwegian groups, and when it was really busy, there was nothing like sitting in the bus door between tours and enjoying a coffee and a smoke. In her opinion, Stockholm was an amazing place. You had the large Swedish royal family with all its interesting personalities and offshoots in every European royal house, not to mention the Stockholm Palace with its endless halls and rooms. She had kept both a fax and an answering machine in case the tourist office happened to call when she was out on a short walk or in case she could not get to the telephone in time.

Inger Becker had also told me that when the police had showed up at Lørens vei 415 early that morning on November 26, 1942, her mother, Dagmar Becker, had told them that she was a Swedish citizen and that she kept a passport at the Swedish legation on Meltzers gate. The policeman had given her mother one hour to retrieve it. Her father, Herman Becker, had already been arrested and taken to Berg. Her mother had called the legation, but there was no one there, so they had fled to Mr. Petersen.[446]

The twenty-five year report for Sinsen High School from 1939-1964 lists all the teachers who worked at the school during that time period. According to this report, Fredrik T. Petersen, born in 1903, Cand.theol.[447] in 1936, taught at the school from 1939 to 1946. There is also a note stating that in 1964 Fredrik T. Petersen changed his name to Riktor.[448] When Dagmar Becker and her children fled to Fredrik T. Petersen, he hid them in a room in his apartment before arranging for a new hiding place and transport to Sweden.[449]

However, I must have misunderstood Inger Becker, because in the archives belonging to the Swedish Ministry of Foreign Affairs, there is a report from the Oslo Consulate General stating that on the morning of November 26, Dagmar Becker filled out a "Form B-Registration," which dealt with Swedish citizenship. On November 30, they had returned and were then supposed to go to the police with the papers, but the embassy had never heard anything more from her. Presumably, it must have been right after November 30[450] that she and her two children sought out Mr. Petersen. Perhaps Inger Becker and her brother had even been at school on Friday the 26th, Saturday the 27th, and Monday the 30th. Perhaps it was then that Mr. Petersen had told her to come to him if anything were to happen. Whatever the case, a few days later, on December 4, they arrived in Sweden and were picked up by Patrol #6 in the "12th patrol area" in Karlstad's military district.[451]

27

Oslo – Auschwitz-Birkenau

IF CLASS WAS held for 2D on the afternoon of November 26, then Hans Kristian Norløff was reading the alleged farewell letter just as the troop transport ship, the *Donau*, was leaving the Oslo fjord.[452]

The Jewish men who had been imprisoned at the Berg detention camp at Tønsberg since October 26 arrived by train from Vestfold. The people who had been arrested in Oslo-area hospitals the previous evening came from Bredtvedt. Not only taxis, but also ambulances and trucks arrived bringing the men, women, and children who were destined to be on board the ship.

The Swedish Consulate General reported to Stockholm that heartrending scenes took place at loading that made a deep impression even on hardened policemen and dockworkers.[453]

The Gettler family and nine members of the Gorvitz family were also on board, as was old Isak Leimann, with whom Elias Lasnik had stayed upon coming to Kristiania in 1908.[454] The men were placed in one cargo hold, the women and children in another.

On November 29, while the *Donau* was sailing for Stettin, Julius and Elise Bassist were married in Stockholm. The couple, who lived at Folkungagatan 144 in the Söder district, thought they had not properly celebrated their wedding in Oslo.

Jenny Bermann, who still lived at a hotel in Stockholm, applied for a leave of absence and a residence permit for Leopold Bermann, so that he could come from the refugee camp in Öreryd in Småland and participate in the festivities.[455]

The bride wore a black dress.[456]

Many who were on board the *Donau* thought that the ship would surely head west and north toward northern Norway as the ships carrying the detained teachers had previously done. The next day, a number of the men pointed out that the ship was following the Swedish coast southward. When it sailed through the Øresund Strait, the *Donau* was so near the Swedish coast that only a couple hundred meters separated it from land. In the southern Swedish province of Skåne, or Scania, lights could be seen in houses and villages, though occupied Zealand in Denmark was completely dark.[457] It was Samuel Steinmann who described all this when he gave a public lecture in January, 2003. Only eight of the 532 *Donau* deportees returned home, and now he was the only survivor left. I arrived early. Since the lecture had been well publicized, I expected it to be well attended. However, there were only about 20 people there. At first I thought there must have been some misunderstanding, since so few people had come. When I had gotten over my initial confusion, though, I realized that 20 people was actually a good turnout when the last survivor from the *Donau* deportation was here to talk about how he had returned alive from Auschwitz. I asked Samuel Steinmann about the Lasnik family, but he did not know them.

He still had his prison uniform, and he showed it to me. According to him, the worst experience he had had during the war had occurred just before the war was over. White buses had arrived from Sweden to collect the Norwegian prisoners. They had driven away, leaving the Norwegian Jews behind.

28

Swedish Diplomats Give It a Try

WHEN THE SWEDISH Consulate General in Oslo reported on November 27 to the Ministry of Foreign Affairs in Stockholm that one Swedish citizen had indeed been deported with the *Donau*, Secretary General Gösta Engzell telegraphed Arvid Rickert, the Swedish ambassador in Berlin. The Secretary General told him that the message concerned an "order from His Excellency" – in diplomatic terms that meant the Minister of Foreign Affairs, Christian Günther – and was occasioned by "the outrageous nature of the deportation measures and the harm this might do to Swedish opinion."[458]

If the deportee or deportees who had ties to Sweden still found themselves aboard the *Donau*, Gösta Engzell hoped that a "démarche," a resolute diplomatic initiative involving a personal inquiry from the ambassador, could at best result in the person or persons being sent to Sweden from the *Donau*'s port of call. However, Engzell added that if they had "already been transported inside of Poland, we fear that there is nothing more we can do."[459] This last comment suggests that the Swedish Minister of Foreign Affairs indeed believed the reports that mass murders by gas were taking place in the Polish concentration camps.

However, the answer from Berlin was discouraging. The ambassador had paid a visit to Dr. Albrecht at the Ministry of Foreign Affairs, where he was informed that the question should be directed to another division. Nonetheless, Dr. Albrecht had promised to look into the matter and had already made the Ministry's political leadership aware of the ambassador's request. Einar von Post from the

Swedish embassy had further explained to the German Ministry of Foreign Affairs that if it indeed turned out that "Swedish subjects or Swedish-born individuals were included in the Jewish transport," no power on earth could prevent Swedish newspapers from harshly criticizing German activities, a move that would prove "harmful to Swedish-German relations."[460]

In the beginning, the German Ministry of Foreign Affairs gave vague answers regarding the release of Jews with Swedish passports and ties. However, when the Swedish diplomats did not back down, a representative of the ministry, H. von Gründherr, explained to Einar von Post that "Foreign Minister von Ribbentrop personally gave the order to German diplomats that if anyone from the Swedish side should make an attempt to interfere in interior Norwegian affairs, all discussion thereof would be rejected as unauthorized meddling." Von Gründherr hoped that no official action, which would "quickly prove harmful to Norwegian Jews," would become necessary.[461] When the Swedish ambassador Arvid Rickert met with von Gründherr about a week later in a final attempt to save the *Donau*-deported Jews with Swedish passports or who were Swedish-born, the German diplomat remarked that it was an example of "typical Jewish manipulations" to suddenly demand Swedish citizenship. "Do you really think it is the case," Herr von Gründherr said, "that German authorities would be willing to let Jews with Swedish ties, who have already been deported, depart for Sweden?"[462]

29

Provisional Gas Chambers

THE *DONAU* LANDED with its cargo of Norwegian Jews at Stettin (now Szczecin) on November 30 at 11:10 a.m. Because of a storm, the voyage had taken a day longer than originally planned.[463] The train carrying the Norwegian prisoners then left Stettin at 2:10 p.m. on the same day.[464] It took a little over 24 hours to arrive at the little Polish city of Oswiecim, or Auschwitz, as it is known in German. The area, which the Germans called Oststreifen, was first occupied and then incorporated into Germany in 1939. The train carrying the prisoners was made up of boxcars and, as one survivor described it after the war, the prisoners "did not have room to sit or lie down, but had to stand. During the whole trip they were not given water and the doors were locked from the outside, so they could not get out in order to relieve themselves."[465] When the train occasionally stopped, cries of "water, water" could be heard from the boxcars. The answer from the outside was always the same: "Jews do not need water."[466] The survivors thought the trip must have lasted for days,[467] but in actuality they arrived at Auschwitz on Thursday, December 1 at 11:00 p.m.[468]

Although Auschwitz eventually became a collective term denoting a system of concentration camps, it is also the name of the first concentration camp in Poland. This camp consisted of ordinary buildings – brick barracks – that had originally housed Polish cavalry. It is this camp that had the famous inscription over the door: "Work Makes You Free." The train carrying the Norwegian Jews stopped midway between Auschwitz and Birkenau. Birkenau, or Auschwitz II, was a much larger concentration camp than the original Auschwitz. There was no inscription proclaiming "Work Makes You Free" over Birke-nau's doors. The barracks, furthermore, were the collapsible stables used by the German army. Sayings such as "Cleanliness is bliss," "Be honest," "Stay neat," and "Truth endures" were painted on beams.[469] Birkenau was located about three kilometers from Auschwitz. The train carrying the prisoners stopped approximately midway between the two camps and the Norwegian Jews exited onto a ramp.[470]

Survivors recounted after the war what happened when the train arrived.

Kai Feinberg: "The moment we were taken out of the car, we were divided into the following two groups: On one side were all the males over sixteen and under fifty years of age. On the other side were all the women and children, together with all the elderly and sick who had been included in the transport. The first group was lined up five by five and carefully counted, while the other group was loaded into cars and sent to a factory-like building, as far as I could see. [...] The factory-like building was none other than a gas chamber and crema-torium. I again want to point out that every woman and child aboard the transport that traveled from Oslo on 11/26-42 was, without excep-tion, sent directly to the gas chamber about twenty minutes after the arrival at Birkenau."[471]

Moritz Kahan: "From Stettin the cargo cars were sent to Auschwitz. Here they were driven up to the camp's platform. They were received by half-drunk SS men equipped with clubs and whips. These under-took a provisional grouping. Women and children (people under the age of 15-16) and those who looked old (over the age of ca. 50) were separated and taken away. In any case, I know that a number of these were stowed in cargo trucks and sent to Birkenau. This took place at night."[472]

Moritz Nachtstern: "Just after arrival at Birkenau, every woman and child was separated and driven away in cars. I asked several pris-oners in the camp where in the world they had been sent. A Polish Jew told me hat they had undoubtedly been sent directly to the gas chamber. The Jew in question worked at the crematorium. This was later confirmed by other prisoners, since the Norwegian women, who were better dressed than most other prisoners, had attracted attention and had been asked where they came from. I had also heard that a few of the really young girls had been separated and sent to a brothel. I, however, cannot vouch for this myself. I assume that all the Jewish women deported from Norway were killed."[473]

There were two so-called provisional gas chambers in use at Birkenau in the fall of 1942. One was in the northwestern and the other in the western corner of the camp. They consisted of two barracks, where the prisoners undressed, and a building with a gas chamber a short distance away. The corpses were cremated in a building just beyond that.[474]

30

Lawyer Haakon Høst Protects Norwegian Interests

LAWYER HAAKON HØST from the Liquidation Board let himself into the Lasnik family's apartment on December 2, 1942. He was accompanied by two appraisers, S. C. Knutsen and Bjarne Russel. "The apartment," they began, "is located in ent. B on 1 fl. and consists of: Comb. dining room and living room w. a fireplace, kitchen, maid's room, bedroom, entryway, restroom, water and wardrobes, as well as a cellar." In the cellar they found two-and-a-half barrels of potatoes, Dora Lasnik's fall potato harvest, collected from her potato patch near the balcony, three bottles of salt, a few jars of rhubarb, and a few other empty containers. As Haakon Høst noted, the combined value of these goods was absolutely nothing.

In the entryway, they registered a mirror with a gilded frame and a coat rack. In the combined living room and dining room, they further discovered oak dining room furniture, a buffet and dining room table with eight chairs – which were, however, "old-fashioned" and "unattractive," according to the attorney. The living room furniture was more to their liking: a Zeitter & Winkelmann piano, a sofa and pillows, lamps and a birch bookcase holding various books. Hanging on the living room wall were "2 ugly paintings," which nonetheless had "nice frames," and in front of the fireplace a trunk with copper fittings.

In contrast, the kitchen contained a new electric "Lyn" stove, an impressive fact, since they were not yet available in stores in December, 1942. Upon inspection, various kitchen appliances were priced at 100 kroner and a note was made that they should be "delivered to Central Collections." The appraisers also found that the bedroom contained birch bedroom furniture, which consisted of two beds, a wardrobe, a small dresser, two bedside tables and two chairs. There was also a cot, a box divan and Dora Lasnik's Singer sewing machine.

When Høst, Knutsen, and Russel came to the hall closet, they found Elias Lasnik's worn-out clothes, eight used women's dresses and three coats. However, because they did not find silverware or jewelry, or any presentable clothes or bedclothes, aside from two old sheets, they concluded that the apartment had already been "stripped." The appraisers also discovered that the veranda door was unlocked and that "Miss Mary Bertelsen lived in the maid's room" as a sublet. Haakon Høst, S. C. Knutsen and Bjarne Russel all signed the document.[475]

Where were Kathe Lasnik's things? Where was her bicycle? The appraisers estimated that the contents of the apartment amounted to 4,310 kroner. That was all: 4,310 kroner. The inventory did not list any of the family's papers and documents, photographs, references or certificates.

S. C. Knutsen bought the piano for 400 kroner, and Major Bakke in Mysen the electric stove. A sofa was sold to Audunson, two armchairs to Ragna Bergs Soldatenheim, a small table to the Front Soldiers' Home in Riis, a birch table to Bruun Evers at Lille Frøensv. 4, an armchair with woolen upholstery to Kjell Assdal at Suhms gate 20, a wardrobe mirror to Frits Ihlen at Vekkerødveien 13, and a birch bookcase to Front Soldier Thoresen at Suhms gate 8, while the bedroom furniture was put into storage for the Front Soldiers' Office.[476]

While the Lasniks' possessions disappeared from within, interest in their apartment mounted from without. The first to make a request was Aage Moe, who had already spoken with lawyer Haakon Høst on December 7, 1942, and who further referenced a conversation with Lieutenant Hanoa of the Ministry of the Police.[477] As it turned out, however, lawyer Egil Reichborn-Kjennerud, the head of the Liquidation Board, had decided on December 10 that the department would go to Chief of Staff Tidemann Ruud.[478] Ruud, though, decided that he would rather have a house than an apartment and so he never moved in. The apartment was then earmarked for Obersturmführer Sveen,[479] who for some reason or other did not move in either. Finally, Egil Holst Torkildsen, the editor of *Germaneren*, moved into the Lasnik family apartment at Hertzbergs gate 7B in February 1943.[480]

Egil Holst Torkildsen tended to leave a large motorcycle, which he would often polish, standing out in the entryway. Apparently, he did not want to take the chance of leaving it outside. This did not prevent some youngsters from eventually putting sugar cubes in the gas tank, however, thereby ruining the motor.[481]

31

Dinner with Terboven

THE ILLEGAL NEWSPAPER *Fri fagbevegelse*, or *Free Labor Movement*, ended its article on the Jewish deportation with the hope that the world might become aware of "these new scandalous German deeds."[482] However, the famous "Voice from London" was silent on the matter; the event was apparently not mentioned in any Norwegian broadcasts in England.[483] Nor did *Meddelelser fra Skipsfartsdirektøren*, the *Announcements from the Director of Shipping*, a publication that brought all types of Norwegian news to sailors, write a word about the deportation of the Norwegian Jews. Still, the Minister of Foreign Affairs, Trygve Lie, received a request from the World Jewish Congress in London on November 27 to ensure that radio broadcasts to Norway would appeal to the population to take whatever means necessary to "prevent the deportation of Jews."[484] However, the Norwegian Minister of Foreign Affairs answered: "Such an appeal is not necessary to rouse the Norwegian population to do its human duty regarding the Jews."[485]

When Swedish diplomats realized it was impossible to save those Jews with Swedish ties who had been deported with the *Donau*, they turned their attention to the Jews still detained in Norway. With this in mind, the Swedish Ministry of Foreign Affairs telegraphed the ambassador in Berlin on December 3 to communicate a request by Prime Minister Albin Hansson: "Quietly make the appropriate arrangements for Sweden to receive all the remaining Norwegian Jews in to prevent them, too, from being deported from Norway."[486]

The Swedish Minister of Foreign Affairs had been approached a few days earlier by a delegation representing the Swedish church. The delegation suggested that the Swedish government approach the Germans and declare that Sweden was willing to take in all remaining Norwegian Jews. The church leaders, furthermore, had contacted the Norwegian legation seeking a guarantee that Norwegian authorities would foot the bill for any Jews evacuated to Sweden. Jens Bull, head of the Norwegian legation, had answered: "In my opinion, it would be more reasonable to expect rich local Jews to support their brethren in times like these, since it is, after all, Jews who are being persecuted." However, Bull believed that this expectation could "without further ado" be dismissed, since "the Jews are Norwegian citizens, after all" and the matter concerned "defenseless people," who "might very well perish in Polish concentration camps."[487]

On December 3, the Swedish Consulate General in Oslo sent a memo to the Ministry of Foreign Affairs in Stockholm. This memo contained a summary of a conversation that one of the diplomats in the Consulate General's Office had had with Hauptsturmführer Wagner, who "in all likelihood is the person on the German side most responsible for the actions against the Jews."[488] The memo also mentioned the nearly 120 Jews who were still imprisoned in Norway and who, for various reasons, had escaped deportation with the *Donau*. The Swedish legation, furthermore, found it significant that Norwegian newspapers had not printed a word about "the latest actions against the Jews, for which neither the German nor the Norwegian authorities seem to want to take full responsibility."[489]

H.R.H. Prince Charles[490] also wrote a plea to the Germans to let the remaining Jews immigrate to Sweden. The plan was that the president of the Norwegian Red Cross, Director F. Heyerdahl, would deliver Prince Charles's letter to the Germans. However, as the Swedish legation reported to the Ministry of Foreign Affairs in Stockholm, Director Heyerdahl had had doubts about this plan: "His first concern was about the political consequences that he believed the matter could have for Sweden." Heyerdahl had also mentioned that the Germans had told him that "it [was] not possible to compromise on the Jewish question," and that the German perspective would tolerate no interference. The Swedish Consulate General in Oslo had subsequently explained to Director Heyerdahl that he did not need to "trouble himself over such considerations, but to leave [the matter] to Swedish authorities." However, Director F. Heyerdahl still had his doubts. Should he deliver the request to the Norwegian authorities or the German ones? This hesitation was due to the fact that "the [two] authorities blamed each other: on the NS side, they have complained about the measures and about their forced cooperation, and on the German side [...] they have complained about the extraordinary foolishness Quisling showed in setting the Jewish persecution in motion." At the same time, Heyerdahl did not want to paint the situation as completely hopeless, because Terboven had also shown "conciliation and a willingness to negotiate" at a dinner he had held for Director F. Heyerdahl and a number of other prominent Norwegians, among them Paal Berg, at Skaugum on December 8.[491]

According to the Swedish Consulate General, Director Heyerdahl thought that about 170 Jews were still imprisoned at various places in Norway, but "especially given the aforementioned dinner," he also thought that "further deportations" could be avoided. The Swedish Consulate General, who did not share Director Heyerdahl's positive view of the situation, wrote to the Ministry of Foreign Affairs that they should try and force Heyerdahl to immediately hand over Prince Charles's letter to the German authorities in Oslo. A few days later, Swedish newspapers referred to Prince Charles's initiative, which had been undertaken together with the Swedish Red Cross. When the matter had leaked out, Heyerdahl finally delivered the letter to the Germans.

The State Commissioner's Office in Oslo, however, rejected the Swedish Red Cross's proposal on the grounds that sending all the Jews who remained in Norway to Sweden did not "comply with the course that the German Reich and the Norwegian government were following with regard to the Jewish question."[492] Accordingly, none of the attempts made by Swedish diplomats bore fruit, and on February 24, 1943, a cargo ship, the *Gotenland*, left Norway with 158 Jews aboard.[493]

The Liquidation Board certainly had its work cut out for it. At the Christmas party on December 20, 1943, lawyer Haakon Høst wrote a song to mark the occasion. After the war, when charges were brought against him, he was again confronted with this song. Of course, he regretted having composed what he called "a piece of trash," but he also added: "That was how it was back then."[494]

Melody: "Lili Marlene"

I.
Once Isaac came from the Mamre plains to Ur
he had just been out on a little tour,
but when he returned to the tent – oh, what dismay –
the tent was empty and Sarah was away.
All had been registered
and speedily transferred.

II.
Then Isaac was sent to the barren Polish land
and Reichborn-Kjennerud took his property in hand.
There was the fatted calf and sparkling glass
and items made of silver and brass.
It was all registered
and speedily transferred.

III.
Then Haakon Høst came with Moses's great book
and preached loud and clear that God gave and God took.
And all that Joseph had amassed
with fraud and cheating unsurpassed
had now been registered
and speedily transferred.

IV.
But all the little tidbits that had not been paid
were what Herr Lindahl eagerly surveyed.

Memos were sent on a grand scale
to Horeb's mount and Jordan's dale
and all was registered
and speedily transferred.

V.
The servants in the vineyard never rested from their work.
God will reward administrators that don't shirk.
If you can work with speed and skill,
you'll be served 'til you've drunk your fill
then you'll be registered
and escorted to your bed.

Lawyer Haakon Høst [495]

Melody: "Lili Marlene" [496]

32

Our Fallen

LAWYER HAAKON HØST, who had been appointed a trustee for the estate of the Lasnik family and 40 other Jewish estates, wrote a statement after the war. In this statement, he claimed that the employees of the Liquidation Board for Confiscated Jewish Property had protected Norwegian interests against the Germans. Therefore, they deserved praise, not prosecution.[497]

He regretted having written the song, but not the letter he had sent to the Ministry of Finance on February 12, 1944, a copy of which was also sent to State Police Chief Karl A. Martinsen:[498] "Regarding the release of the Jewess Elise Bassist born Lasnik's assets." It irritated Haakon Høst that on December 21, 1942, Minister-President Vidkun Quisling had decided that her estate should be released, because she had become a Swedish citizen by marriage on October 26, 1942. It appears, namely, that the industrious Haakon Høst had already sold all the inventory and goods contained in her shop to Johs. Leborg & Co. The contents of Hertzbergs gate 7, moreover, were spread to the four winds. Haakon Høst characterized the Minister-President's decision as a "deplorable blunder"[499] resulting from the Ministry of Internal Affairs' exclusive focus on the fact that she had become a Swedish citizen – "which [itself] should be doubtful enough." He then referred to a conversation with Vidkun Quisling regarding this matter, wherein the Minister-President had admitted that the release of Elise Bassist's assets was first and foremost a "friendly 'gesture' to the Swedes" and that "one perhaps therefore had not looked too closely at the question of when and how they had become Swedish citizens."[500]

Such a "friendly gesture" was, in Haakon Høst's opinion, unlawful, and was "in any case partly [...] a gift." And how had this gift been received? he asked rhetorically. By Elise Bassist threatening through lawyer Chr. Blom to sue the state for damages: "One could say that Swedish citizenship has not changed little Elise's Jewish mentality when it comes to business affairs!"[501]

In the treason case against Haakon Høst in 1945, Judge Erik Solem – who had been a leading figure in the resistance movement, so much so that the NS gave him the nickname "Erik Blood-Axe"[502] – asked if it were true that Haakon Høst had acquired "a number of personal objects belonging to Jews who either fled or were sent to Germany, or the proceeds from the sale of said objects. Is it the case that you appropriated such things?"

Høst: "I did not view it like that, because the objects I either received or sold would be accounted for when the estates were accounted for. [...]"

Judge: "Was it your intention to give them back?"

Høst: "No, not when I received them. But after the surrender, when I was hiding in the woods, I drew up an exact account, so that I could settle up."[503]

Eventually, lawyer Haakon Høst was found guilty of the liquidation of lawyer Kaare Schetelig, a resistance fighter, and sentenced to death in the Eidsivating Court of Appeals.[504] In an appeal and defense statement he wrote to the Supreme Court after the verdict, Haakon Høst gave a new interpretation of the song he had written for the Liquidation Board's Christmas party. After the party had gotten "a little animated," one of the secretaries had said that they should make up a song about the bosses. The suggestion had been met with general applause, and so Haakon Høst, together with an "older employee," had written the song in 45 minutes: "None of us realized that we had incorporated the Jew's tragedy in a tasteless way – the idea was simply to give the employees an easy way to poke fun at their bosses."[505]

Lawyer Haakon Høst also wrote that he had let an older Jewish couple remain at Deichmans gate 21 after having made an official visit to them at the end of February, 1943. To his surprise, however, he had received the keys to the apartment not long after; on the back of the envelope was written the name of Assistant Police Chief Knut Rød. The couple had been deported on the *Gotenland* to Germany on February 23, 1943.[506] As Haakon Høst continued: "I do not make mention of this as a 'good deed' that could clear my name," but because he found it strange that "[t]he man whose name was on the back of the envelope, and who, together with the Germans, directed the State Police's Jewish campaign in the fall of 1942, is being released today, according to what two stunned detectives have told me – since his situation was resolved at Christmas in 1945 by a prominent government official."[507]

A month before Haakon Høst visited the couple at Deichmans gate, however, NS Attorney General Sverre Riisnæs wrote to State Police Chief Karl A. Martinsen that no one "could draw attention to a couple of Jews who were about to be overlooked"[508] except Haakon Høst. In making this statement, he was specifically talking about the couple at Deichmans gate 21.

Lawyer Haakon Høst's appeal was ultimately denied, although he died in a hospital before his sentence could be carried out.[509]

Knut Rød not only went free, but after a while he was even reinstated in his job at the Oslo Police Department. Dr. Hans Eng, the State Police doctor, was also able to get back to work, although his return was not as quick and painless as Knut Rød's had been. According to the indictment, Hans Eng was "an especially fanatic and persistent Nazi."[510]

The indictment against him included the effort he had made to arrest hospitalized Jews.[511] Since the document filled six pages, the prosecution thought that they had enough on him. He had attended executions in order to sign the death certificate, among these the execution of two deaf-mute individuals. On the way to another execution, he had sat next to the person condemned to death and had said: "I might as well go ahead and sit next to the corpse."[512]

On December 13, 1948, Hans Eng was sentenced to seven years in jail. He was released on probation on December 12, 1949, and pardoned on March 3, 1950. At his pardon, he was given permission to "practice medicine in secondary hospital positions or in needy districts, according to further determination by the Director General of Health [...]." In January 1952 he again received "the right to practice medicine."[513]

Knut Rød was ultimately acquitted by the Eidsivating Court of Appeals on February 4, 1946. The Attorney General challenged the verdict, and in August of that same year the Supreme Court annulled the acquittal. On April 9, 1948, the case again came before the Eidsivating Court of Appeals. Again, Knut Rød was acquitted. On May 8, almost a month later, he tried to win back the position he had held at Oslo's Criminal Police Division in 1940, but the selection committee rejected his application. Knut Rød then sued the police by way of the Ministry of Justice, and on September 10, 1949 the Oslo City Court delivered a unanimous verdict: Knut Rød was entitled to resume the position he had occupied before the war.[514]

Haakon Høst was not the only person astounded by the fact that Knut Rød, the man who had not only organized the Jewish arrests in the Oslo area, but had also handed the Jews over to the Germans at Pier 1, could be acquitted after the war.[515] Hauptsturmführer Wilhelm Wagner was the German who directed the Norwegians regarding the arrests and who took charge of the Norwegian Jews meant for the *Donau*. In his statement, he said that if he had refused to do any of this, he would have been shot or sent to a German concentration camp.[516] Wilhelm Wagner's argument that he had acted under duress would not land him an acquittal. Indeed, most people who were charged with participating in the persecution of Jews claimed that they had been forced to do so by their superiors. One logical consequence of the duress argument, of course, is that there is actually only one person, or at most one small circle around Adolf Hitler, who was responsible for the campaign to exterminate the Jews of Europe. The duress argument, in fact, presupposes that an individual who is being forced to do something against his or her will must, in turn, force another person to do something against his or her will, and so on. If that were true, though, would the Jewish arrests and deportations have been carried out as effectively as they were in Norway?

The duress argument also fails as a valid explanation in another way. After the large-scale police actions of October 26 and November 26, 1942, there were no complaints that a significant number of people neglected to show up to carry them out. Although force can be used to counter resistance, it does not appear that any such threat was needed to motivate the individuals who arrested the Norwegian Jews in the fall of 1942. Karl A. Martinsen never reported that many of the men called in from the State Police, nor the 60 men from the Oslo Criminal Police, nor the 100 men from the Oslo Emergency Department, nor the 100 requisitioned taxis, showed any reluctance to take part, not to mention failed to appear. The Swedish authorities, furthermore, recorded the names, occupations, and addresses of all Norwegians to cross the Swedish border. It is clear from these lists that the men who had been conscripted to work for the Germans fled in droves. However, only one policeman from Oslo crossed the border in the fall of 1942: Jon Martinus Røyland.[517]

Knut Rød was charged under Section 223 of the Penal Code, which states that "any person who unlawfully deprives another of his liberty or aids and abets such deprivation of liberty" can be punished. This Section was applicable to everyone who took part in the actions against the Jews, even if the individuals involved did not know what would happen to the Jews after they were sent to Germany. In both judgments handed down by the Court of Appeals, Knut Rød was acquitted, however, because the court approved of the fact that he had supported the enemy "purely with the intention of camouflaging his extremely important work in favor of the resistance movement and the Home Front."[518] That is, the court accepted that Knut Rød had organized the Jewish arrest to conceal his more important efforts on behalf of the resistance movement. At the same time, the arrests in Oslo and Aker were a huge and difficult undertaking that, as Karl A.

Martinsen put it, had to be "carried out like a battle and within a very short period of time."[519]

The first acquittal of Knut Rød was not a unanimous decision. As Judge Cappelen put it: "There is no evidence that the accused – when he was faced with these crimes – had to fulfill patriotic duties of such weight and so inextricably linked to his position in the State Police that his leading role in the arrests of the Jews can be justified."[520] He did not accept the camouflage argument, namely, but asked: what actions supporting the resistance movement could have been so momentous that they outweighed the deportation of the Jews? What good could possibly outweigh such evil?

The policemen who took the stand on behalf of Knut Rød had themselves participated in the arrests of the Jews. Indeed, they were the ones who used the camouflage argument. However, as an explanation for what ended up being an extremely effective and professionally carried out police action, the camouflage argument does not hold up.

State Police Officer Leif Strenge Næss was among those who took part in the arrests on October 26, 1942. He and Michael Berg from the German SS made up patrol unit #3.[521] However, his written statement is unclear: "The police group, who practically speaking were in contact with almost all the illegal organizations in Oslo, were warned about all the actions against the Jews. The State Police group was not supposed to do anything apart from alerting the police group. That was according to the orders we had had to go on from the beginning. I'm convinced that Løvstuhagen got the orders for the first police action against the Jews from Rød."[522]

Added to this, State Police Officer Petter Kittelsby and State Police Officer Mathias Løvstuhagen together gave a written statement explaining their relationship to Knut Rød. The explanation, however, contains nothing that supports the idea of a general warning going out before the campaigns against the Jews began. Moreover, Løvstuhagen and Kittelsby both participated in the campaigns against the Jews. An addendum from Petter Kittelsby simply states that he had the definite impression that Rød "did not do more than he was forced to do by the Germans and State Police Chief Martinsen."[523] Here, the duress argument instead of the camouflage argument makes an appearance.

According to the written statements given by Leif Strenge Næss, Petter Kittelsby and Mathias Løvstuhagen, Knut Rød did know that there was a resistance group in the State Police Department. Apparently, he supported the group by passing along information. However, what type of support he gave and what kind of information he passed along is not specified in the written documents. When asked to join the group, Knut Rød refused.

Knut Rød did give an extremely detailed account of his involvement with the campaigns against the Jews. What he wrote, however, does not support Leif Strenge Næss's assertion that Rød was the origin of the general warning that preceded the Jewish arrests. If he did warn the people he knew worked for the resistance movement, why did he not declare that fact in his defense statement? At the same time, Knut Rød did mention a few actions he took in support of the movement. However, these actions were insignificant in comparison to the claim of a warning that "practically speaking, went out to all the illegal organizations in Oslo." Among other things, Knut Rød apparently wanted a Jew, "Cantor Bodd," to escape. To see that happen, he "was ready to take some risks, but I was reluctant to tell him that directly."[524] Despite his intimations, however, Jacob Bodd was deported on the *Donau*. Knut Rød also mentioned a Jewish woman "from the neighborhood" whose husband had been arrested. According to his statement, she sought him out when she also heard that the "Jewish women were to be detained. She asked for advice." Supposedly, Knut Rød confirmed that the women would indeed be detained and concluded his description with the assertion that he could provide her name. However, he also wrote: "I demand that she not be called as a witness."[525] Why not? As it turns out, before Knut Rød wrote his statement at Ilebu on September 16, 1945, he had indeed contacted the woman and asked her if she would act as a witness on his behalf when his case went to court. However, she had said no, because she had felt as though she had had to squeeze the information out of him.[526] Finally, Knut Rød's brother, who wrote "A statement on Master of Law Inspector Knut Rød's Activities for the State Police,"[527] mentioned nothing about a general warning being issued to the State Police resistance group prior to the campaign against the Jews. At the same time, his brother also maintained that Knut Rød had kept him updated on all his work during the war.

After the Supreme Court had considered the Attorney General's challenge and decided to overturn Knut Rød's acquittal,[528] the case again came before the Court of Appeals on April 9, 1948. This time the judge was the feared Erik Solem, and the verdict was unanimous. Knut Rød was acquitted. The court favorably viewed the fact that "[h]e joined the NS solely with the idea that, under cover of membership, he could perform work useful to his country, and that is indeed what he did."[529] Furthermore: "When the court considers the defendant's activities as a whole, it cannot find evidence that the defendant in reality offered the enemy support of any consequence. Those actions that, taken by themselves, could be regarded as supporting activities, were necessary so that he could carry out his much more important resistance work."[530] Regarding the campaign against the Jews, Erik Solem decided that Knut Rød had not "acted of his own initiative, but was following orders. If he had refused to participate, it would not have made any difference, except that then he would not have had the opportunity to exercise the moderating influence that was possible on the business."[531] However, the written documents from the case again fail to give examples of the important resistance work that Knut Rød supposedly carried out. Could it be that the fact that the Home Front had eyes and ears in the State Police was so important that it cancelled out Rød's participation in all other types of activity?

As Knut Sveri, a sociologist of law, puts it: "It gives me the uncomfortable feeling that the court did not see Norwegian Jews as equal to other Norwegians." He then points out the fact that State Police employees who were also members of the Home Front had all taken part in the Jewish campaign and "must have had a personal interest in presenting the activities of the illegal cells – including Rød's – in the best possible light."[532] Knut Sveri also takes into account the fact that Erik Solem, who also occupied important positions in the Home Front, thus had a particular perspective on the business. Indeed, as Sveri continues, one cannot "discount the possibility that a man like Rød, whom the organized resistance movement saw as reliable, was acquitted for protecting the Home Front's reputation."[533]

For his part, Knut Rød does not claim to have joined the NS in order to camouflage his resistance work, but rather to prevent NS troops from receiving police assignments. As Knut Rød asserts in his statement, that would have been "the worst thing that could happen." Instead, it was "seemingly better to join the NS, so that veteran policemen from before the war could continue their work."[534]

Kolbjørn Rød paints his brother's membership in the Nasjonal Samling in a similar light. Apparently, the experienced officers in the Criminal Police all agreed that they should join the organization, so that their division would not end up "pervaded with active NS members." Knut Rød claimed that it was both possible and important to uphold a procedurally correct and professional police force during the occupation. Indeed, that was the very reason he did not join the organized resistance movement. To join the movement would have conflicted with a certain ideal – namely, that of a policeman who managed to maintain a purely professional and technical perspective. For the same reason, he had been "reluctant" to directly advise Cantor Bodd that he should flee to Sweden.

As a result, Knut Rød used the professional argument to justify his actions. He claimed that his intention to maintain a professional and workman-like police environment should exempt him from criminal liability. That was Knut Rød's main argument. As a result, the duress argument and the camouflage argument played a lesser role in his written statement. When his first acquittal was overturned, he wrote a new defense statement: "Had I [...] by chance taken the rest of my summer vacation during the week of November 22 through 29, instead of November 1 through 8 – which well could have happened – I would have assuredly avoided the events surrounding the

Donau's departure."[535] Here Knut Rød makes his participation in the Jewish campaign a question of pure chance. Even in hindsight, it was unthinkable to him that he could have either refused to participate or simply left the country. A professional policeman does not behave in that way.

With regard to the duress argument, however, how was Knut Rød able to quit the police force on September 14, 1943, and to leave the Nasjonal Samling later that same month[536] if the argument has any validity? And if the camouflage argument indeed motivated Knut Rød's actions to some extent, why did he quit either organization in the first place?

The only explanation for the ability of Norway to carry out two extremely effective Jewish campaigns was the existence of a professional, seemingly independent Norwegian police force, which enjoyed a certain legitimacy with the population, and to which the Germans could give direct orders. And yet, why did the police follow those orders and arrest Norwegian Jews? In the end, the campaigns against the Jews proved to be so effective because those who could have resisted participated. Knut Rød took part because he believed that it was better that the work be carried out by professionals, rather than Hirden.[537] The members of the Home Front participated because they wanted to camouflage what they considered to be more important – namely, their resistance work.

Kathe Lasnik's Square, 2011

A park-like area in the district of Oslo where the greatest number of Jews had lived was named "Kathe Lasniks plass" – Kathe Lasnik's Square – in 2011.

When I began working on the book about Kathe Lasnik, I never thought it would prove so difficult to find sources. Though she only reached 15 years of age, she had spent her life in Norway's capital city, where she lived in apartment buildings with lots of neighbors and attended large, centrally located schools with hundreds of fellow students. The purpose of this book was to reconstruct her life, and in doing so to tear her loose from the embrace of those monuments that could only tie her to the extermination. However, as it turned out sources were all but nonexistent, and those that did exist were also tied to the arrest and extermination. What did this lack of sources reveal? Could that very lack itself be considered a source of something – and if so, what? It was only long after I had written the book that I could piece together this line of reasoning and answer this question. The lack of sources goes to show just how effective the attempt to eradicate Oslo's Jewish population was. It was not simply murder, but rather all-out extermination.

That it was nonetheless possible to write a description of Kathe Lasnik's life is due to a number of institutions and people. The National and City Archives in Oslo – the National Archives, the State Archives and the Oslo City Archives; Deichmanske Library; Statistics Norway's Library; Norway's Resistance Museum; the National Archives in Stockholm; the Panstwowe Muzeum, Auschwitz-Birkenau w Oswiecimiu; Oslo Commercial High School; Fagerborg School; Oslo Coppersmiths' and Tinsmiths' Guild.

Kathe Lasnik's two surviving sisters, Jenny Bermann and Elise Bassist, also contributed in many ways, first by answering my questions when I visited them. After that, Jenny Bermann answered questions relayed through her daughter, Faye Speert, and Elise Bassist through her daughter, Dorrit Liberman. I also owe heartfelt thanks to Jenny Bermann's son, Ivar, Kathe Lasnik's classmates from the girls' class 1-5A (1934-1938) at Møllergata School, the students from the girls' class 5-7C (1938-1941) at Majorstua School and the students from the middle school class 1-2D (1941-1942) at Fagerborg School, as well as to the children from Hertzbergs gate and Suhms gate 1938-1942, who also provided valuable information. Who contributed which information can be found in the footnotes.

Nonetheless, I assumed that when the book was published, it would awaken other memories and put me in contact with people who knew more about Kathe Lasnik. That was indeed the case and that is what I will write about here. However, something also happened that I had not foreseen. A number of people who experienced the persecution of Jews contacted me and recounted what had happened to other individuals, as well as their own experiences. Among others, I came into contact with a man who said he was in possession of a wartime diary. It was a diary written by a young Jewish girl. When he told me that, the impossible flashed through my mind – but no, it was Rosa London who had kept a little pocket diary during 1942, 1943, and 1946. I had no idea that there were other eyewitness accounts – a written contemporaneous document, no less – from the persecution of Jews.

Rosa London was born in 1911 and lived at Markveien 64, vis-à-vis Anna Lasnik's store at number 58. It seems that she began keeping a diary in the spring of 1942 because she had fallen in love with a man: "E," as she calls him in the diary. On Friday, May 15 she writes that E called and invited her out on both Friday and Saturday. She had thanked him, but declined. On Sunday, May 17 they were together at Frognerseteren. "Really nice," she wrote. On Tuesday, May 19, E called, and on Thursday, June 4, he called again. They planned to meet on Saturday. On Thursday, June 23, she writes that E called two times.

However, in the fall of 1942, the entries in her pocket diary come to concern other things. On Monday, October 26, 1942, both Rosa London's father and E are arrested. The following day she delivers a packet to Bredtvedt prison with clothes and medicine. On Thursday, October 28, she pays a visit to the police and is told that the men have "traveled to Tønsberg." On Saturday, October 31, she delivers a packet to the Red Cross for E and "papa" with a set of underclothes, three handkerchiefs, a sleeping bag, a pair of gloves, and a cap. That same Saturday she travels to Tønsberg. On Thursday, November 17, a man named Koren came to inventory the furniture in the apartment; his appraisal was low, she writes: piano 2,000 kroner, living room furniture 250 kroner, a bookshelf with books 125 kroner, dining room furniture 1,200 kroner. Wednesday, November 25, she writes: "Got information at 10 o'clock that women and children will be arrested." She and nine others went into hiding and they crossed into Sweden at 3:30 a.m. on November 28. Rosa London's boyfriend, E, did not return home from Germany. After the war, she married a man who had survived internment in Auschwitz-Birkenau.

Moritz Gorvitz supplied information about tinsmithing for the book, and he was at the press conference when the book was launched. When I visited him just before Christmas, he showed me a notebook with a poem. He told me that he had had it with him at the press conference, and that he had intended to read aloud an insulting poem he had written about Quisling and performed for his fellow prisoners at Berg concentration camp. "But you should've gone ahead and done it," I said. "I wouldn't have been able to," Moritz Gorvitz replied, "I would've started crying." One of Mauritz Gorvitz's brothers was named Bjarne; a friend of his, Ivar Thorsheim, wrote an article about him at the turn of 2003/04. The title reads: "My classmate: Bjarne Gorvitz, Born: July 5, 1925. Died: Auschwitz, November 26, 1942." Thorsheim made 40 copies of the article. Among others, he sent it to some of the members of the boys' class at Bekkelaget Elementary School who were still alive. The five-page article was about playing and school and about how Bjarne Gorvitz had started working in his father's tinsmith workshop on Arups gate in Gamlebyen after he finished elementary school in 1939.

Many of the people who lived at Wilses gate 6 also contacted me and told me all about the apartment building, about the bath and sauna located in the basement, and about a dentist named Strandrud who had an office in the same third-floor apartment that the Lasnik family vacated in 1927, right before Kathe Lasnik was born. A woman who had moved into the building in 1948 said that Mrs. Strandrud still managed a dentist's office on the third floor. She also told me about her grandfather, who had been a taxi driver and had helped Jews cross the Swedish border during the war. She did not know much about it and added that maybe it was not such a big deal after all, since after the war she heard that many Norwegians earned good money by helping out in that way.

Hans A. Strandrud was the grandson of Tore O. Strandrud, who purchased Wilses gate 6 from Abraham Josef Korizintsky in 1919. He said that his grandfather had earned quite a bit on real estate speculations in Rjukan and had invested in Wilses gate 6 in Kristiania. He also had quite a bit of information about the building and its inhabitants, among other things a complete account book from the interwar period. He remembered that his mother, who was born in 1912 and grew up on Mariboes gate, had once mentioned that there had been a Jewish family on Wilses gate who had never returned.

Randi Olsen, who was born in 1911 and had been friends with Anna Lasnik, telephoned me. Part of the large family across the corridor, she was 15 years old and an errand girl when Kathe Lasnik was born. She recounted how the children in the two families had gone to each other's birthday parties. Randi Olsen had brought chocolates – that was what they gave each other on such occasions. She bought them for a few øre in one of the small tobacco and chocolate shops where they were sold by weight. They also got tissue paper at the store; it had nice, bright colors and was shredded up. They packed the pieces of chocolate in the paper and then put them into a box or a cone. When she was telling the story about the birthday gift, I thought of

Jenny Bermann. She wanted a box of Kong Haakon Chocolates from Norway, her son told me. "I like having something like that to pass around when there are guests," she said when I gave it to her in Boston in 2001. She had remembered the old days, maybe the interwar period on Wilses gate, when the young girls paid each other birthday visits and brought chocolates wrapped in tissue paper. Randi Olsen tried to describe how the tissue paper with nice colors had been cut into strips or shredded. The girls had thought it was so pretty; they had kept it and had used it to play with. Randi Olsen also said one of her brothers had been an assistant to Elias Lasnik when he had his workshop on Karl Johans gate in the early 1920s.

Jan Erik Hægh managed to find a picture of Kathe Lasnik. The family had had a cabin in Berger on Nesodden. In one of his mother's albums was a photograph from a summer day in 1934 or 1935. His mother had written "London Bridge is Falling Down" over it. The picture shows a then 7- or 8-year-old Kathe Lasnik together with the brothers Jan Erik and Tor Hægh. Tor Hægh and Kathe Lasnik are the ones trying to trap Jan Erik Hægh.

A woman in Lunner in Hadeland thought she knew the farm where Kathe Lasnik and Inger Becker spent one summer. All I had done was repeat Inger Becker's description of the road to the train station, the steps down to the small lake where they swam, the house in which they had stayed, which had stood a little apart from the others, and the farmhouse with its large veranda. It was there that they had eaten dinner and looked out over the sea. The farm's name was Nedre Ulven and it was right next to Vassjø, a lake; the train station was called Grindvoll. She had also looked in a local history book and indeed it mentioned that Nedre Ulven had received summer guests.

I talked to the people who live on the farm today. Melvin Blekkerud could verify that the farm had indeed had some kind of guest facilities, but there were no documents, pictures or archives that could tell us anything more. Blekkerud also said that one vacationing guest at the farm, a tinsmith, had added a bell tower to the storehouse in 1939.

I figured that it must have been Elias Lasnik. The family could have vacationed at the farm in 1939, and so Kathe Lasnik and Inger Becker had been there in the summer of 1940. Blekkerud said that there had been Jews there, among others one by the name of Hurwitz, a magician with the stage name Ben Hur. It had been the summer farm out in Nordmarka that he had rented. There he had relaxed and fished from early in the morning until late at night.

Anita Østern, now Stenklev, had met Kathe Lasnik in the winter of 1939. She is in the picture with the white anemones, as well as in the picture of the children posing with their bikes outside of her entryway at Hertzbergs gate 3A. One of the first times they had gone out and played, Kathe Lasnik had followed Anita Østern home: "I have to tell you something," she'd said with a serious face, "I'm Jewish." Anita Østern had just answered, "Yeah." After that they never mentioned it again. Anita Østern was an only child, while Kathe Lasnik was a child born much later than her siblings. So they were friends, even though Anita Østern was a grade above Kathe Lasnik. Anita Østern told me that one time she had gotten a new pink dress. Kathe Lasnik had liked it so much that she'd asked where the dress came from. Miss Lauksund on Schønings gate had sewn it. Kathe Lasnik had gone to the seamstress on Schønings gate and gotten a nearly matching pink summer dress. Anita Østern's father, a lawyer and the Second Secretary in the Ministry of Trade, came home from his office at 12 o'clock on "panic day," April 10, 1940. They hitched a ride with a truck up to Sognsvann. The Østern family did not have their own place to visit outside of the city, but an acquaintance who had already evacuated had loaned Mr. Østern a villa in Berg. The family stayed there the entire spring. Kathe Lasnik went to Anita Østern's almost every day. They picked white anemones. They played records at Bjørg Tutta Hansen's apartment on Suhms gate. Bjørg Tutta Hansen's aunt had given her a hand-cranked phonograph and a large collection of Swedish records. In 1940 the favorite had been Alice Babs's "Swing It, Magistern!" with lyrics by Hasse Ekman and melody by Kai Gulmar.

On Saturdays the Lasnik family ate boiled chicken, and Anita Østern thought the way her friend's family got together every week for that meal looked very cozy. One Midsummer's Eve during the war, either in 1941 or 1942, the Second Secretary in the Ministry of Trade took his family and his daughter's friends for sandwiches at Dronningen, Oslo's most popular summer restaurant, which was located on Frognerkilen bay. That was certainly an experience.

The two girls often walked to school together, and one day, Anita Østern thought it might have been in the spring or fall of 1942, Kathe Lasnik said: "We've got an invitation to move to America, what do you think?" Anita Østern did not know how to answer the question. She didn't think it was a good idea for Kathe to leave. At that point, it would have been impossible to get from Norway to the United States anyway.

Anita Østern had heard nothing about the slip of paper or letter that Kathe Lasnik had written and left behind when she was arrested. However, that was not the case with Dagny Dutheil, born Nilsen. She had lived at Kirkeveien 129 and her father was the manager of a lumber company. She was in the same middle school class as Kathe Lasnik at Fagerborg School. During the fall of 1942, the school had borrowed some classrooms at Foss School up in Grünerløkka, and they had often walked to school together. After the book came out and she heard about the letter, Dagny Dutheil was indignant. The letter had not been written in that cursory telegram style; it had been much warmer. And so she related what she had experienced on the morning of November 26, 1942.

When Dagny Nilsen had swung down Hertzbergs gate in order to walk with Kathe Lasnik across Blåsen, Alexander Kielland's Square, and onwards to Foss school, Edith Gjeruldsen, the friend from whom Kathe Lasnik had collected her jacket and had borrowed a suitcase, came running: "Dagny, Dagny, you should take the letter."

Edith Gjeruldsen does not remember that. Was it someone else who gave Dagny Nilsen the letter? At any rate, when she learns what happened early that morning, she runs all the way to school, goes up to the teacher's desk and gives the paper to Hans Christian Norløff, saying that it is a farewell letter from Kathe Lasnik. She notices that Mr. Lorløff reads it first, before she goes and sits down, and then he reads it out loud to the class.

Her classmate and friend remembers that Kathe Lasnik had been anxious. One time, when they were walking to school together, she said that her father was in the hospital. She wanted to have him home again. That might have been after her two sisters had crossed over to Sweden with their husbands. "Oh, Dagny," she had exclaimed, "you're lucky to be Norwegian. The Germans don't hate you. The Germans hate us Jews."

Most of the students had taken pictures in the summer of 1942. It was Dagny Nilsen who delivered the list with the orders for extra copies to the photographer at Fridjof Nansens Square. Kathe Lasnik had told Dagny Nilsen that she was very interested in Steinar Steinarsson, and had asked Dagny to give him a picture afterwards. Dagny Nilsen has always wondered what Kathe Lasnik meant by that. Afterwards. After what, exactly?

Kathe Lasnik Year by Year

1908   Elias Lasnik (b. 1887) and Dora Meszansky (b. 1888)
come to Kristiania

1909   The couple marry, live at Grünersgate 5

1909   Jenny Lasnik born at Markveien 28 on December 4

1911   Anna Lasnik born November 19

1913   Elise Lasnik born at Wilses gate 6 on December 31

1927   Kathe Lasnik born at Wilses gate 6 on October 13

1931   The Lasnik family members become Norwegian citizens
on May 26

1934   Kathe Lasnik enters class 1A at Møllergata School on April 21

1936   Family moves to Fredensborgveien 2 on April 21

1937   Jenny Lasnik marries Leopold Bermann on November 7

1938   Kathe's nephew Ivar Bermann born on August 3
Family moves to Hertzbergs gate 7B on December 15

1939   Kathe Lasnik enters class 5C at Majorstua School
on January 4

1941   Graduates from elementary school on June 22
Enters Class 1D at Fagerborg School on August 18

1942   Takes her final exam for class 1D on June 22
Begins in class 2D on August 18
Leopold Bermann flees to Sweden on October 25
Elise Lasnik marries Julius Bassist and becomes a Swedish
citizen on October 26
Elise and Julius Bassist travel to Sweden on November 7
Jenny Bermann and her son flee to Sweden on November 15
Elias Lasnik is arrested at Lovisenberg Hospital
on November 25
Kathe Lasnik is arrested together with her sister, Anna
Lasnik, and her mother, Dora Lasnik, on November 26
Died, Birkenau, on December 1

Notes

1. The National Unification Party, or Nasjonal Samling (NS), was a Fascist party in Norway from 1933-1945.
2. The journal *Samfunnsspeilet* 4/98, Oslo 1998.
3. William Seltzer, "Population Statistics, the Holocaust, and the Nuremberg Trials," *Population and Development Review*, Vol. 24. No. 3 Sept. 1998.
4. Arne Ording, Gudrun Johnson Høibo, Johan Garder (eds.), *Våre falne 1939-1945*, Pub. by Den norske stat. Oslo 1949-1951, Vol. III, p. 115.
5. Booklet, Oslo, n.d.
6. Handbook for the National Archives, Oslo 1992, p. 293.
7. Street addresses have been retained in the original. "Gate" means street, "vei" means road.
8. *Statistical Reports*, Central Bureau of Statistics 10.6-12, 1948.
9. Document collection on "The Deportation of Jews from Norway to Auschwitz," comp. by T. Friedmann, August 1963, Haifa, 13, 38, 46.
10. Danuta Czech, *Auschwitz Chronicle, 1939-1945*, Trans. Barbara Harshav, et al., Henry Holt & Co., New York 1990.
11. The city of Oslo was named Kristiania in the period from 1624 to 1924.
12. Folder 16, Box 10, Jews in Oslo, Campaigns against the Jews, State Police, Ministry of the Police 1940-45, National Archives.
13. Registry card for Elias Lasnik, Oslo Population Register, Regional State Archives, Oslo.
14. Interview Elise Bassist.
15. Gérard Silvain and Henri Minczeles, *Yiddishland*, Gingko Press, Corte Madera 1999, 9.
16. Moses Rischin, *The Promised City, New York Jews 1870-1914*, Harvard U. Press, Cambridge 1962, 270.
17. Ibid., 77.
18. Gérard Silvain and Henri Minczeles, ibid., 34f.
19. The Russian Jews in 1905 through the Eyes and Camera of a British Diplomat, Tel Aviv University, Tel-Aviv 1986 14f.
20. Ibid., 21f.
21. Interview Elise Bassist.
22. *Salmonsens konversationsleksikon*, Second Edition, Vol. XXV, København MCMXXVIII, 187f.
23. Gene S. Meiran, Meszansky/Lasnik Family Tree, interview Elise Bassist.
24. Ibid., interview Irene Levin.
25. Interview Elise Bassist.
26. Annual Census in Kristiania on February 1, 1909, Akersgaten 73, Oslo City Archives.
27. Ibid., Thorvald Meyers gt 26.
28. Wullf Meszansky, Annual Census 1900, Historical Data Center. www.rhd.uit.no/folketellinger.html.

29. Annual Census in Kristiania on February 1, 1909, Akersgaten 73, Oslo City Archives.

30. Ibid., Seilduksgt 9.

31. Ibid., Eilert Sundts gt 53.

32. Ibid., Thorvald Meyers gt 26.

33. Instructions for the Annual Census in Kristiania on February 1, 1909, Oslo City Archives.

34. Norsk Lovtidende, 1901, 2. sec., p. 195f. Cited here from Sander Tufte, *Norwegian Foreign Politics 1901-1927, Legislation and the Practice of Rejection*, Dissertation at the Historic Institute, University of Oslo, fall 2000.

35. Kristiania Address Book 1909.

36. Ibid.

37. *Norway's Official Statistics*. v.167. Haandverkstællingen in Norway 1910. First booklet. Enterprises, Independently Employed Craftsmen and Workers. Kristiania 1912. Table 3.

38. Tinsmiths' Association. *40 Years' Report Oslo*. Ed. by H. Guneriussen, Oslo 1935, pp. 18 and 31.

39. Norway's Official Statistics. v.147. Fabrikstællingen in Norway 1909, Second booklet. Workday in Industry. Table 3. p. 206.

40. *Statistical Yearbook for the City of Kristiania*. Pub. by the Municipal Statistics Office 1911. Table 56.

41. The Israeli Congregation, Register E Marriage Ceremonies, p. 142. The Mosaic Religious Community's Archives, Oslo City Archives.

42. Ibid.

43. The Israeli Congregation, Register A: New members of the congregation, p. 20. The Mosaic Religious Community's Archives, Oslo City Archives.

44. Oskar Mendelsohn, *The History of the Jews in Norway for 300 Years*, Vol. 1 1660-1940, Oslo 1987, p. 678.

45. Marta Gjernes, ibid., p. 50.

46. Oskar Mendelsohn, ibid., p. 433.

47. Marta Gjernes, ibid., p. 39.

48. Oslo Population Register, Registry Card for Elias Lasnik, Regional State Archives, Oslo.

49. Registry Card for Elias Lasnik, Oslo Population Register, Regional State Archives, Oslo.

50. Annual Census in Kristiania on February 1, 1910, Markveien 28, Oslo City Archives.

51. Interview Elise Bassist.

52. Registry Card for Elias Lasnik, Oslo Population Register, Regional State Archives, Oslo.

53. Annual Census in Kristiania on February 1, 1910, Markveien 28, the Oslo City Archives.

54. *Statistic Yearbook for the City of Kristiania*. Pub. by the Municipal Statistics Office 1915. Table 108.

55. Kenneth T. Jackson (ed.), *The Encyclopedia of New York City*, New Haven & London 1995, p. 1282f.

56. Marta Gjernes, ibid., Annex 3.3.

57. Eivind Saxlund, *Jews and Goyim*, Kristiania 1922, 1st edition 1910, 2nd edition with excerpts from the press debate in 1911 and 1912.

58. *Aftenposten*, January 24, 1911.

59. *Dagbladet*, January 29, 1911.

60. Tinsmiths' Association. *40 Years' Report*. Ed. by H. Guneriussen, Oslo 1935, p. 40f.

61. *Oslo Tobacco Workers' Association 1881-1951*, Oslo 1951, p. 31f.

62. The Most Popular Girl's Name from 1880-1917. www.ssb.no/navn.

63. Annual Census in Kristiania on February 1, 1913, Wilses gate 6, Oslo City Archives.

64. Ibid.

65. Interview Elise Bassist.

66. Annual Census in Kristiania on February 1, 1913, Wilses gate 6, Oslo City Archives.

67. Mara Gjernes, Lecture March 20, 2003. Center for Studies of Holocaust and Religious Minorities in Norway.
68. Building Archives, Fire Assessment, Wilses gate 6, Oslo City Archives.
69. Building Archives, Drawings, Wilses gate 6, Oslo City Archives.
70. Annual Census in Kristiania on February 1, 1913, Wilses gate 6, Oslo City Archives.
71. Oskar Mendelsohn, *The History of the Jews in Norway for 300 Years, Vol. 1 1660-1940,* Oslo 1987, p. 337.
72. Annual Census in Kristiania on February 1, 1913, Wilses gate 6, Oslo City Archives.
73. Registry Card for Elias Lasnik, Oslo Population Register, Regional State Archives.
74. Kristiania Tax Office, Main Register, Oslo Population Register, Regional State Archives.
75. *Household Accounts for a Number of Lower Income Families in Kristiania, Bergen, Trondhjem, Drammen, Kristiansand and Hamar in the Years 1912/13.* Pub. by Kristiania Municipal Statistics Office, Kristiania 1915. Table 3, p. 84.
76. Ibid., p. 91.
77. Annual Census in Kristiania on February 1, 1913, Wilses gate 6, Oslo City Archives.
78. Ibid.
79. Norway's Official Statistics. x. 178. Statistical Overviews 1948, Table 192.
80. Annual Census in Kristiania on February 1, 1913, Wilses gate 6, Oslo City Archives.
81. Joh. Søhr, *Spies and Bombs: From the Investigative Police Department's Operations During the World War,* Oslo 1938, p. 11.
82. Ibid., p. 27.
83. Kristiania Tax Office, Main Register 1914/15, Oslo City Archives.
84. Ibid., 1915/16, 1916/17.
85. Ibid., 1917/1918, 1918/19, 1919/20.
86. Interview Elise Bassist.
87. Ibid.
88. Annual Census in Kristiania on February 1, 1920, Wilses gate 6, Oslo City Archives.
89. Annual Census in Kristiania on December 1, 1921, Wilses gate 6, Oslo City Archives.
90. Annual Census in Kristiania on December 1, 1922, Wilses gate 6, Oslo City Archives.
91. Oslo Tax Office, Main Register 1920/21, Oslo City Archives.
92. *Fifty Years of the Oslo Coppersmiths' and Tinsmiths' Guild: An Account of the Guild's Operation 1884-1934,* pub. on the occasion of the 50th Anniversary, June 30th 1934, Oslo 1934, p. 39.
93. Skilled Trades Act. July 15, 1913. No. 11. Chapter 2, Section 13.
94. Interview Elise Bassist.
95. *Periodical for Norway's Coppersmith and Tinsmith Masters' League,* No. 2, 1924, p. 10ff.
96. Board Minutes, Members' Meeting, November 12 1920, Kristiania Coppersmith's and Tinsmith's Guild, Oslo Coppersmith's and Tinsmith's Guild.
97. Ibid., Annual Report 1920, Kristiania, December 13, 1920.
98. Interview Moritz Gorvitz.
99. Oslo City Court, 0087 Court Records 7/9/20-19/3/21, p. 381f., Regional State Archives, Oslo.
100. Ibid., p. 382.
101. Ibid.
102. Residency Book for Elias Lasnik, j.nr. 2423. Packet marked "1931 j.nr. 2401-2700," Citizenship Papers, Ministry of Justice, National Archives.

103. Oslo City Court, 0087 Court Records 7/9/20-19/3/21, ibid.
104. Board Minutes, Board Meeting, 21/9-21, Kristiania Coppersmiths' and Tinsmiths' Guild, Oslo Coppersmiths' and Tinsmiths' Guild.
105. Ibid.
106. Interview Elise Bassist.
107. Kristiania Tax Office, Main Register 1921/22, Oslo City Archives.
108. Ibid., 1922/23, 1923/24.
109. Ibid., 1924/25.
110. Interview Dorrit Liberman.
111. Interview Elise Bassist.
112. Interview Dorrit Liberman.
113. *Statistical Yearbook for Oslo 1926*, pub. by the Municipal Statistics Office. Table 61.
114. Borgerskolen Public School, School Tuition, Fb-0008, IVD, Oslo City Archives.
115. Borgerskolen Public School, Grades, Fa-0013, IVD, Oslo City Archives.
116. School Tuition Register, Form. courses 1925-26, Oslo Commercial High School.
117. *Oslo Commercial High School: Annual Report for the Fifty-first School Year 1925-26.* Oslo 1926, p. 15f.
118. Møllergata School, School Records, 1915-39 and 1943, Oslo City Archives. Examination Records, 1926-27, 2E, Oslo Commercial High School.
119. Møllergata School, Registration and Graduation Register 1917-1965, Oslo City Archives.
120. Hammersborg School, R-Accounts 1918-1933, Oslo City Archives.
121. Interview Elise Bassist.
122. Hammersborg School, F-Student Affairs, Student Registers, Grades. 1925-1935. F 0015, Oslo City Archives.
123. Interview Elise Bassist.
124. Ibid.
125. Ibid.
126. Interview Jenny Bermann.
127. Interview Elise Bassist.
128. Annual Census in Oslo on December 1, 1928, Wilses gate 6, Oslo City Archives.
129. Ibid.
130. Oslo Address Book 1928.
131. Registry Card for Kathe Lasnik, Register of Aliens 1928-1939, Central Passport Office 1917-1957, National Archives.
132. Register A, New members of the congregation, 1921, p. 37. The Mosaic Religious Community, Oslo City Archives.
133. Register C, Live Births, 1927, p. 85. The Mosaic Religious Community, Oslo City Archives.
134. *The Norwegian School in Uppsala 1941-1945*, Oslo 1970, pp. 116, 120.
135. Interview Elise Bassist.
136. Annual Census in Oslo on December 1, 1927, Wilses gate 6, Oslo City Archives.
137. Building Archives. Building Number 208, Property Registration 823, Oslo City Archives.
138. Interview Dorrit Liberman.
139. Interview Elise Bassist.
140. *Statistical Yearbook for the City of Oslo*. Published by the Municipal Statistics Office 1928. Table 52.
141. Annual Census in Oslo on December 1, 1928, Fredensborgveien 25, Oslo City Archives.
142. Interview Moritz Gorvitz.
143. Annual Census in Oslo on December 1, 1928, Wilses gate 6, Oslo City Archives.
144. Ibid.
145. Ibid.
146. Oslo Tax Office, Main Protocol 1927/28, Oslo City Archives.
147. *Statistical Yearbook for the City of Oslo*. 1928, p. 101.

148. Oslo Tax Office, Main Protocol. 1928/29, 1929/30, Oslo City Archives.

149. Ibid.

150. Building Archives, Building Report, Building Number 208, Property Registration 823, Oslo City Archives.

151. *Norwegian Encyclopedia of Artists,* Vol. 1, Oslo 1982, p. 391.

152. Interview Aslaug Ligård.

153. Oskar Mendelsohn, *The History of the Jews in Norway for 300 Years,* Vol. I 1660-1940, Oslo 1987, pp. 337, 362.

154. *Aftenposten,* June 9, 1926, cited from Per Ole Johansen, *Watching Out For Ourselves: Norway and the Jews 1914-1943,* Oslo 1984, p. 64.

155. *Proceedings in Odelstinget,* 1929, p. 578.

156. *Proceedings in Odelstinget,* 1927, p. 1109, cited from Per Ole Johansen, ibid., p. 69.

157. J.nr. 2432. Packet marked "1931, 2401-2700," Certificates of Citizenship, Police Office, Ministry of Justice, National Archives.

158. Oskar Mendelsohn, *The History of the Jews in Norway for 300 Years,* Vol. I 1660-1940, Oslo 1987, p. 431.

159. Jr.n. 2423, ibid.

160. Ibid.

161. Registry Cards for Elias Lasnik, Dora Lasnik, Elise Lasnik, Kathe Lasnik, Registry of Aliens 1928-1939, Central Passport Office 1917-1957, National Archives.

162. Registry Card for Elias Lasnik, Oslo Population Register, Regional State Archives, Oslo.

163. Act No. 3 of 8 August 1924 relating to Norwegian citizenship, Section 2.

164. *Statistical-Economic Overview of the Year 1931,* prepared by Central Bureau of Statistics, p. 3.

165. J.nr. 2423, ibid., Oslo Tax Office, Main Register I 1931/32, Oslo City Archives.

166. Interview Elise Bassist.

167. Oslo Tax Office, Main Register 1930/31 and 1931/32.

168. Interview Elise Bassist. Folder 15, Box 10, Jews in Oslo, Persecution of Jews, State Police, Ministry of the Police 1940-45, National Archives.

169. Interview Elise Bassist.

170. Oslo Address Book 1932.

171. Ibid.

172. Annual Census in Oslo on December 1, 1932, Wilses gate 6, Oslo City Archives.

173. Interview Dorrit Liberman.

174. Norway's Official Statistics. XII 245. Historical Statistics 1968, Table 57.

175. Oslo Address Book 1934.

176. Annual Census in Oslo. Ibid.

177. Ibid.

178. *Oslo Address Book* 1933.

179. Letter from the Norwegian Ambassador in Berlin to the Foreign Ministry on April 27, 1933. Cited here from Erik Bråthen, *Defensive Politics as Jewish Refugee Politics: The Politics of the Scandinavian Countries Confronted with History,* Historical Institute, University of Oslo, spring 1999, p. 45.

180. Ibid., p. 44.

181. Ibid.

182. *Aftenposten,* editorial, April 4, 1933. Cited here from Per Ole Johansen, *Watching Out For Ourselves,* Oslo 1984, p. 99f.

183. Annual Census in Oslo on December 1, 1934, Brogaten 6, Oslo City Archives.

184. Oslo Address Book 1933.

185. Annual Census in Oslo on December 1, 1933, Wilses gate 6, Oslo City Archives.

186. Oslo Tax Office, Main Register, 1923/33, 1933/34, Oslo City Archives.

187. Interview Jenny Bermann.

188. Annual Census in Oslo on December 1, 1933, Wilses gate 6, Oslo City Archives.

189. Norway's Official Statistics. X. 178. Statistical Overviews 1948, Table 192.

190. Interview Anne Marie Kolloen.

191. Report on Oslo Elementary Schools, Reform Schools and Continuation Schools for the School Year August 1st 1924 until July 31st 1925, prepared by Oslo School Board Office, p. 12. Report on Oslo Elementary Schools, Reform Schools and Continuation Schools for the School Year August 1st 1934 until July 31st 1935, prepared by Oslo School Board Office, p. 12.

192. *Norwegian Encyclopedia of Artists*, Vol. 3, Oslo 1986, p. 89.

193. Hagtor Traavik (ed.), *The Downtown School: Møllergata School 1861-1961*, Oslo 1961, p. 132.

194. Report on Oslo Elementary Schools, Reform Schools and Continuation Schools for the School Year August 1st 1932 until July 31st 1933, prepared by Oslo School Board Office, p. 23.

195. Report on Oslo Elementary Schools, Reform Schools and Continuation Schools for the School Year August 1st 1934 until July 31st 1935, prepared by Oslo School Board Office, p. 27.

196. Report on Oslo Elementary Schools, Reform Schools and Continuation Schools for the School Year August 1st 1935 until July 31st 1933, prepared by Oslo School

Board Office, p. 16. Register 1A: Møllergata School, Oslo City Archives.

197. *The Downtown School: Møllergata School 1861-1961*, Oslo 1961, p. 132. Report on Oslo Elementary Schools, Reform Schools and Continuation Schools for the School Year August 1st 1932 until July 31st 1933, prepared by Oslo School Board Office, p. 23.

198. Møllergata School, Fi-Journals, 1912-1939, Fi 0008, Oslo City Archives.

199. Interview Synnøve Vinje and Aslaug Ligård.

200. Møllergata School, Fi-Journals, 1912-1939, Fi 0008, Oslo City Archives.

201. Oslo Tax Office, Main Register 1934/35, Oslo City Archives.

202. Annual Census in Oslo on December 1, 1935, Wilses gate 6, Oslo City Archives.

203. *Journal of Norway's Coppersmith and Tinsmith Masters' League*. No. 2 1929, p. 10.

204. Annual Census in Oslo on December 1, 1935, Akersveien 21, Oslo City Archives.

205. Oslo City Court, Police and Justice Cases: Record of Judgment no. 156, September 14, 1934, Regional State Archives, Oslo.

206. Oslo City Court, Police and Justice Cases: Record of Judgment 163, November 2, 1935, Regional State Archives, Oslo.

207. Interview Elise Bassist.

208. Annual Census in Oslo on December 1, 1935, Wilses gate 6, Oslo City Archives.

209. Interview Elise Bassist.

210. Annual Census in Oslo on December 1, 1935, Wilses gate 6, Oslo City Archives.

211. Interview Elise Bassist.

212. Møllergata School, Fi-Journals, 1912-1939, Fi 0008, Oslo City Archives.
213. Interview Aslaug Ligård.
214. Interview Aslaug Ligård and Synnøve Vinje.
215. Interview Eva Kristine Skaug.
216. Report on Oslo Elementary Schools, Reform Schools and Continuation Schools for the School Year August 1, 1935 to July 31, 1936, produced by Oslo School Board Office, p. 8 and 14.
217. Ibid., p. 29.
218. Ibid., p. 40.
219. Interview Aslaug Ligård.
220. Programs and brochures for May 1, 1936. Labor Movement's Archives.
221. *Arbeiderbladet*, May 2, 1936.
222. Interview Karin Johanne Skoglund.
223. Oslo Tax Office, Main Protocol: 1935/36, Oslo City Archives.
224. Annual Census in Oslo on December 1, 1936. Fredensborgveien 2, Oslo City Archives.
225. Ibid.
226. Report on Oslo Elementary Schools, Reform Schools and Continuation Schools for the School Year August 1, 1935 to July 31, 1936, prepared by the Oslo School Board Office, p. 27.
227. Interview Aslaug Ligård.
228. Report on Oslo Elementary Schools, Reform Schools and Continuation Schools for the School Year August 1, 1936 to July 31, 1937, prepared by the Oslo School Board Office, p. 48.
229. Interview Karin Johanne Skoglund.
230. Nic. Stang, "Around 1940 – and the Legend of the Norwegian Resistance," *Kontrast* 2 1966, p. 57.
231. Interview Karin Johanne Skoglund.
232. Ibid.
233. Interview Eva Skaug.
234. Interview Aslaug Ligård.
235. Oslo Tax Office, Main Register: 1936/37, Oslo City Archives.
236. Elisenberg Hospital, Journal Elias Lasnik, Oslo City Archives.
237. Møllergata School, Fi-Journals, 1912-1939, Fi 0008, Oslo City Archives.
238. Annual Census in Oslo on December 1, 1937. Fredensborgveien 2, Oslo City Archives.
239. Oslo Tax Office, Main Register 1937/38, Oslo City Archives.
240. Oslo Address Book 1938.
241. Registry Card for Elias Lasnik, Oslo Population Register, Regional State Archives, Oslo.
242. Oslo Tax Office, Main Register 1938/39, Oslo City Archive.
243. Report to the Tax Inspector in Oslo from Account Inspector C. Brække on Book Inspection Held on 12/10-1940, Folder 95/C, Box 955, Reparations Office for Confiscated Assets 1942-50, National Archives.
244. *Statistical Yearbook for the City of Oslo 1941*, pub. by the Municipal Statistics Office. Table 9.
245. *Oslo City Encyclopedia*, 4th ed., Oslo 2000.
246. Record Book for E. Lasnik's Apartment in Hertzbergs gate 7, December 22, 1942, Folder 95/C, Box 955, Reparations Office for Confiscated Assets 1942-50, National Archives.
247. Ibid.
248. Annual Census in Oslo on September 15, 1940, Hertzbergs gate 7, Oslo City Archives.
249. *Majorstua School 1908-1958*, Oslo 1958, p. 225f.

250. Character Certificate Register, 1941, Class 7C. Majorstua School, Oslo City Archives.

251. Interview Elise Bassist. Registration Form, Folder 95/C, Box 955, Reparations Office for Confiscated Assets 1942-50, National Archives.

252. Interview Elise Bassist.

253. Interview Celia Gorlén.

254. Ibid.

255. Ibid.

256. Interview Jannicke Eckhoff.

257. Interview Fride Wilhelmsen.

258. Registration Records 0001, 1926-1939, Majorstua School, Oslo City Archives.

259. Oskar Mendelsohn, *The History of the Jews in Norway for 300 Years*, Vol. 1 1660-1940, Oslo 1987, p. 650f.

260. http://www.vaksinepakken.org/joder/fenster.html.

261. Oskar Mendelsohn, *The History of the Jews in Norway for 300 Years*, Vol. 2 1940-1985, Oslo 1987, p. 238.

262. Interview Inger Becker.

263. Ibid.

264. Odd Hølaas, *Norway Under Haakon VII*, Oslo 1945, p. 408.

265. Interview Inger Holtung.

266. Interview Dorrit Liberman.

267. Journal for Elias Lasnik. Med. dept. Lovisenberg GB-023, admitted by Dr. O. Jervell, journal recorded by Dr. Dalaker. Diakonissehuset Hospital Dept. V, Oslo City Archives.

268. *Aftenposten*. Evening ed. Oslo, Thursday, April 9, 1940.

269. Annual Report on Oslo Elementary Schools, Boarding Schools and Continuation Schools for the School Year July 1, 1939 - June 30, 1940, p. 39.

270. Nils Johan Ringdal, *Between a Rock and a Hard Place: The Police During the Occupation*, Oslo 1987, p. 16.

271. *Lofotposten,* Svolvær, Wednesday, April 10, 1940.

272. Interview Edith Lunder.

273. Interview Elise Bassist.

274. Folder 11. File 413, Box 8, Jewish Campaigns, State Police Archives. Police Department 1940-45, National Archives.

275. Application for Residence Permit June 25, 1940, National Board of Aliens, Registry Office, m. vol. F1ABA:351 Central Dossier for Jenny Bermann, National Archives of Sweden.

276. Application for Residence Permit June 25, 1940, National Board of Aliens, Registry Office, m. vol. F1ABA:351 Central Dossier for Leopold Bermann, National Archives of Sweden.

277. Majorstua School: Teacher Council Minutes 1908-59, Oslo City Archives.

278. Annual Report on Oslo Elementary Schools, Boarding Schools and Continuation Schools for the School Year July 1, 1930 - June 3, 1940, p. 39f.

279. Interview Turid Vizcarra.

280. *Norwegian War Encyclopedia 1940-45*, Oslo 1995.

281. Folder 95/C, Box 955, Reparations Office for Confiscated Assets 1942-50, National Archives.

282. Per Ole Johansen, *Watching Out For Ourselves: Norway and the Jews 1914-1943*, Oslo 1984, p. 136f.

283. Administrative Council's Meeting Minutes with Addendum. From 4/15/1940-9/25/1940, Meeting Report, May 16, 1940, National Archives. Cited here from: Per Ole Johansen, ibid., p. 138f.

284. Administrative Council's Meeting Minutes with Addendum. From 4/15/1940-9/25/1940, Meeting Report, May 16, 1940, National

Archives. Cited here from: Per Ole Johansen, ibid., p. 139f.

285. Oskar Mendelsohn, *The History of the Jews in Norway for 300 Years*, Vol. 2. 1940-1985, Oslo 1987, p. 18. The Jewish community in Oslo received the letter from the Oslo police on May 15, while the communication on August 7 came from the German Security Police. Mendelsohn does not provide any reference for the letters.

286. Bjarte Bruland, lecture January 27, 2003.

287. P.M. reg. Norwegian Subject, medical doctor, Dentist Leopold Bermann, Stockholm June 5, 1940. National Board of Aliens, Registry Office, m. vol. F1ABA:351 Central Dossier for Leopold Bermann, National Archives of Sweden.

288. Application to the National Board of Health and Welfare, Residency Permit, June 25, 1940, National Board of Aliens, Registry Office, m. vol. F1ABA:351 Central Dossier for Leopold Bermann, National Archives of Sweden.

289. Application to the National Board of Health and Welfare, Residency Permit, June 25, 1940, National Board of Aliens, Registry Office, m. vol. F1ABA:351 Central Dossier for Jenny Bermann, National Archives of Sweden.

290. Journal for Elias Lasnik, Med. Div. Lovisenberg GB-023, Diakonissehusets Hospital Division V, Oslo City Archives.

291. National Board of Health and Welfare to the Office of the Governor of Stockholm July 9, 1940, National Board of Aliens, Registry Office, m. vol. F1ABA:351 Central Dossier for Leopold Bermann, National Archives of Sweden.

292. P.M. to National Board of Health and Welfare. Stockholm, Criminal Police Station, 8/19, 1940, ibid.

293. Folder 11. File 413, Box 8, Campaigns against the Jews, State Police Archives. Ministry of the Police 1940-45, National Archives.

294. Oskar Mendelsohn, *The History of the Jews in Norway for 300 Years*, Vol. 2. 1940-1985, Oslo 1987, p. 16.

295. Report to the Tax Inspector in Oslo from Account Inspector Sigurd Widerøe on Book Inspection held on 3/29-1943. Folder 95/C, Box 955, Reparations Office for Confiscated Assets 1942-50, National Archives.

296. Income Tax Return 1940, Elise Lasnik, ibid.

297. Meeting Minutes 0001 Teachers' Council. 1908-1959, Majorstua School, Teachers' Council 8/19, 10/14, 1940, Oslo City Archives.

298. Teachers' Council 11/9, 12/11, 1940, ibid.

299. Character Certificate 7C/p, 1941, Character Certificate Register 002, 1936-1945. Majorstua School, Oslo City Archives.

300. Interview Randi Elton.

301. Teachers' Council 1/21, 1941, ibid.

302. Interview Randi Elton.

303. Teachers' Council 2/7, 1941, ibid.

304. Herlof Kløvstad (ed.), *Sinsen High School, 1939-1964*, Oslo 1964, p. 15.

305. Teachers' Council 2/7, 1941, ibid.

306. Interview Inger Holtung.

307. Interview Helga Haugen.

308. Carl Falkstrøm, *Stockholms Tidning*, May 17, 1941. Cited here from *Announcements from the Director of Shipping*, June 19, 1941. No. 23, p. 4f.

309. *Svenska Dagbladet*, May 24, 1941. Cited here from *Announcements from the Director of Shipping*, April 10, 1941. No. 18, p. 25.

310. Annual Report on Oslo Elementary Schools, Boarding Schools and Continuation Schools for the School Year July 1, 1940 - June 30, 1941, p. 57.

311. Character Certificate 7C/p, 1941, Character Certificate Register 002, 1936-1945. Majorstua School, Oslo City Archives.

312. Annual Report, ibid., p. 46.

313. Character Certificate Register 002, ibid.

314. Annual Report, ibid., p. 44f.

315. Character Certificate Register 002, ibid.

316. Interview Helga Haugen.

317. Directive 8.5.1942, Ministry of the Police / State Police Division, National Archives, Oslo.

318. *Norwegian War Encyclopedia 1940-45*, Oslo 1995.

319. Ibid.

320. Oskar Mendelsohn, *The History of the Jews in Norway for 300 Years*, Vol. 2. 1940-1985, Oslo 1987, p. 9.

321. *Norwegians in Captivity 1940-45*, Oslo 1995.

322. *The Encyclopedia of Jewish Life Before and During the Holocaust*, Vol. III, New York 2001, p. 1401.

323. Interview Elise Bassist.

324. Viggo Barfoed, *Fagerborg School 1916-91: 75 Years*. Oslo 1990, p. 20f.

325. Character Certificate Register 002, 1936-1945, Majorstua School, Oslo City Archives. Protocol Class 1D 1941-42, Fagerborg School.

326. National Bibliography, Theses at Norwegian Universities 1906-1989. www.nb.no/baser/.

327. Draft of School Council Register, August 1941-11/13 1959, Fagerborg School.

328. Register of Grades 1937/38-1943/44, School Year 1941/42 1D, Fagerborg School.

329. *Fritt Folk*, National Organ for Nasjonal Samling, September 10, 1941.

330. Harald Berntsen, *Two Lives -- One Fate. Viggo Hansteen and Rolf Wickstrøm*, Oslo 1995, p. 358.

331. J.nr. 5289/41A, Chief of the Criminal Police. Jews in Norway – reg., Ministry of the Police 1940-45, National Archives.

332. J.nr. 00182/1942A, ibid.

333. J.nr. 99182/1942A, ibid.

334. J.nr. 3888/1941A, ibid.

335. J.nr. 3808/41A, Draft of letter dated 10/15-41 and with inscription "To the interpreter! The present matter should not lie long.", ibid.

336. Directive, Stamping of Jews' Identity Cards, January 19, 1942, J.nr. 5289/41A.

337. Interview Edith Lunder.

338. Letter from Nasjonal Samling's Statistics Agency to County Executive Axel Aas, Drammen, Oslo January 16, 1942, L-sak Oslo pkm, p. 3549, National Archives.

339. Addendum no. 1 (pr. January 1942) to the provisional inventory (pr. December 1941) of Jewish businesses in Norway, ibid.

340. Letter from Nasjonal Samlings' Statistics Agency to Herr Kaptein Langlie, Oslo January 10, 1942, ibid.

341. To the State Police Chief. J.nr. 1205/42B, Registration of Jews in Norway, Ministry of the Police, National Police Chief, L-sak Oslo pkm., D 4094, National Archives.

342. Report to Oslo Police Station, Department of Collaborators. Pub. by Assistant Detectives Thorbjørn Frøberg and Knut Eberling, Oslo, October 4, 1946, ibid.

343. Instructions, Questionnaire for Jews in Norway, Oslo February 6,

1942, J.nr. 1205/42B, Ministry of the Police 1940-45, Jews in Norway – reg., National Archives.

344. Doc. 12, p. 6. L-sak Oslo pkm, p. 3549, National Archives.

345. Questionnaire 407, 408, 409, 410. Folder 16, Box 10, Jewish Arrests, State Police Archives, Ministry of the Police 1940-45, National Archives.

346. School Council January 23, 1942, School Council Register, August 1941-11/13 1959, Fagerborg School.

347. Hans Fredrik Dahl, *Vidkun Quisling: A Leader on the Precipice,* Oslo 1992, p. 369.

348. *Norwegian War Encyclopedia 1940-45,* Oslo 1995.

349. Annual Report on Oslo Elementary Schools, Boarding Schools and Continuation Schools for the School Year July 1, 1939 - June 30, 1940, prepared by the Office of the School Board, Oslo 1943, p. 4.

350. Viggo Barfoed, *Fagerborg School 1916-91: 75 Years,* Oslo 1990, p. 31.

351. Ibid.

352. School Council May 7, 1942, School Council Register, August 1941-11/13 1959, Fagerborg School.

353. *Norwegians in Captivity 1940-1945,* Oslo 1995.

354. Final Exam 1D, Register 1941/42, Fagerborg School.

355. Interview Jon Andreas Reiersrud.

356. F. M. 25 1/5 The Jewish Question, Vol. 1. Minister Finn Koren to FM London August 17, 1942, National Archives. Cited here from Ole Kolsrud, "Exile-Norway and the Jews During World War II," *Historisk Tidsskrift*, Vol. 73, No. 3 1994, p. 303.

357. Express telegram from the State Police Chief to the Norwegian police authorities, dated October 26, 1942. File marked: STAPO

C II B 2. Folder insert marked: Jewish Federation, State Police, Ministry of the Police 1940-45, National Archives.

358. Organizational chart of the German Security Police in Norway, Interrogation of Wilhelm Wagner 4.12 1945. L-sak Oslo pkm. D 2479, National Archives.

359. Report on the Arrest of Male Jews over 15 Years Old in Oslo, by an officer in the State Police, Oslo and Aker Division, dated November 5, 1942. Journal labeled: OV 5000/41. RA, Folder marked: Jewish Campaigns STAPO, State Police, Ministry of the Police 1940-45, National Archives.

360. Ibid.

361. Knut Rød's Commentary to the Report to the Oslo Police Station, Department of Collaborators. Pub. by Assistant Detectives Thorbjørn Frøberg and Knut Eberling, Treason Division, L-sak Oslo pkm. D 4094, National Archives.

362. The Campaign against the Jews. Catalog of Patrols. Chief of the Criminal Police. Jews in Norge – reg., Ministry of the Police 1940-45, National Archives.

363. Catalog of Patrols, ibid., and Confiscation Form 205, Lasnik, Elias, Folder 30, Box 16, Jewish Arrests, State Police, Ministry of the Police 1940-45, National Archives.

364. Confiscation Form 205, ibid.

365. The Jewish Campaign. Catalog of Patrols, ibid.

366. Form for Confiscation, Number 413, Leopold Berman, October 26, 1942, Jews in Norway -- reg., Chief of the Criminal Police, Ministry of the Police 1940-45, National Archives.

367. Interview Elise Bassist.

368. Nils Johan Ringdal, *Between a Rock and a Hard Place: The Police During the Occupation*, Oslo 1987, p. 235. Oskar Mendelsohn, *The History of the Jews in Norway for 300 Years*, Vol. 2. 1940-1985, Oslo 1987, p. 81.

369. Oskar Mendelsohn, *The History of the Jews in Norway for 300 Years*, Vol. 2. 1940-1985, Oslo 1987, p. 79.

370. Journal for Elias Lasnik, L.nr. 1725/1942, J.nr. 90/XI. Lovisenberg Hospital, Oslo City Archives.

371. Koppom in Järnskog District Attorney's Office on October 26, 1942, Dnr. 13266/42. National Board of Aliens, Registry Office, m. vol. F1ABA:351 Central Dossier for Leopold Bermann, National Archives of Sweden.

372. Kx nr. 3172, 17/11 1942, Headquarters, Swedish Defense Staff, Foreign Department, Ministry of Foreign Affairs, 1920 Year's Dossier System, HP 1970-1972, National Archives of Sweden.

373. National Board of Aliens, World War II Camp Archive, Registry Card Leopold Bermann, no. vol DI:3, National Archives of Sweden.

374. Oskar Mendelsohn, *The History of the Jews in Norway for 300 Years*, Vol. 2. 1940-1985, Oslo 1987, p. 87.

375. Document 19, p. 6., L/sak Oslo pkm. 4094, National Archives.

376. Report on the Arrest of Male Jews over 15 Years Old in Oslo, by an officer in the State Police, Oslo and Aker Division, Dated November 5, 1942, Journal labeled: OV 5000/41. RA, Folder marked: Jewish Campaigns STAPO, State Police, Ministry of the Police 1940-45, National Archives.

377. Court Record for Oslo City Court September 9, 1949, p. 1. L-sak Oslo pkm. D 4094, National Archives.

378. Reg. 662, 10.20.1942, HP, 31, An, UD, 1920 Years' Dossier System, HP 1070-1072, National Archives of Sweden.

379. Ibid.

380. Reg. 850, 11.25.1942, HP, 31, An, UD, 1920 Years' Dossier System, HP 1070-1072, National Archives of Sweden.

381. Ingvar Svanberg & Mattias Tydén, *Sweden and the Holocaust: Debates and Documents on Europe's Jews 1933-1945*, Stockholm 1997, p. 236.

382. Göran von Otter to Legation Secretary Lagerfelt, London July 23, 1945, Ministry of Foreign Affairs, 1920 Years' Dossier System, HP vol. 1051, National Archives of Sweden.

383. Paul A Levin, *From Indifference to Activism: Swedish Diplomacy and the Holocaust, 1938-1944*. Acta Universitatis Upsaliensis. Studia Historica Upsaliensis, Stockholm 1996, p. 129.

384. P.M. Stockholm September 7, 1942, HP, 21, I, Ministry of Foreign Affairs, Policy Department Cases HP 217, Volume 1049 (1935-1943), National Archives of Sweden.

385. Paul A. Levin, ibid., p. 127.

386. Ibid., p. 129f.

387. Ink d 11/6 1942, Dnr H:1761, Karlstad's Defense Area to Headquarters, Swedish Defense Staff, Foreign Department, Ministry of Foreign Affairs 1920 Years' Dossier System, HP 1970-1972, National Archives of Sweden.

388. Interview Inger-Johanne Østerbø.

389. Interview Elise Bassist.

390. Application to Vidkun Quisling from the Interim Church Leadership November 19, 1942. Cited here from Oskar Mendelsohn, *The History of the Jews in Norway for 300*

Years, Vol. 2. 1940-1985, Oslo 1987, p. 100f.

391. Journal for Elias Lasnik, L.nr. 1725/1942, J.nr 90/XI. Lovisenberg Hospital, Oslo City Archives.

392. Note dated Stockholm 11/30-1942, signed Koritzinsky, "Jews in Norway 1940-42," L-sak Oslo pkm. D 2479, National Archives.

393. Physician Statements for Sick Jews, 5000/42, No. 205, State Police, Jewish Campaigns. The Arrest of Jews in Oslo. National Archives.

394. Ibid.

395. Report to the State Police Chief, given by Constable R.A. Hansen, 11/17 1942, Jewish Campaigns. The Arrest of Jews in Oslo, 5000/52, nr. 205, State Police, Ministry of the Police 1940-45, National Archives.

396. Report to the State Police Chief, given by Constable F. Myhrvold, 18/11 1942, ibid.

397. National Board of Aliens, Registry Office, m. vol. F1 ABB:2737, Central Dossier for Edvard Syvertsen Interrogation Rep. D.nr. 14 047/42, Report on November 15, 1942, National Archives of Sweden.

398. National Board of Aliens, World War II Camp Archive, Registry Card Leopold Bermann, no. vol DI:3, National Archives of Sweden.

399. Interview Inger Holtung.

400. Interview Steinar Olav Steinarsson.

401. Folder 30, Box 16, Jewish Campaigns, State Police, Ministry of the Police 1940-45, National Archives.

402. Act relating to the Confiscation of Jewish Assets. Announced October 29 in *Lovtid*. 1 no. 55.

403. Confiscation Form for Elias Lasnik with inscription "Liquidator: Haakon Høst," Folder 26, Box 15, Jewish Campaigns, State Police, Ministry of the Police 1940-45, National Archives. Doc. 27. Advocate Haakon Høst's Explanation to Investigator Ruth at the Reparations Office for Confiscated Assets. L-sak Oslo pkm. H. 3335, National Archives.

404. Doc. 7, L-sak Oslo pkm. H 3335, National Archives, Oslo.

405. Ibid.

406. Ibid.

407. Ibid.

408. Ingvar Nielson to Haakon Høst November 18, 1942. File 94/C, Box 955, Reparations Office for Confiscated Assets, National Archives.

409. Rental Record for Markveien Kitchen Supplies, ibid.

410. D.V. Sundsten to Haakon Høst November 24, 1942, ibid.

411. Inventory Trondhjemsveien Kitchen Supplies, ibid.

412. Lawyer Haakon Høst to the Liquidation Board, January 21, 1943, ibid.

413. A/S Stormbull, Invoice 06295, 10/23/1942, Inscription "to be sent to the property executor 17/11/42," ibid.

414. Interview Elise Bassist.

415. Creditor List, ibid.

416. *Aftenposten*, November 24, 1942.

417. Martinsen's own words in the note "Evacuation of Jews, Oslo, on November 27, 1942," Oslo pkm., L-sak D2479, National Archives.

418. *Document Collection on "The Deportation of Jews from Norway to Auschwitz,"* comp. by T. Friedmann, Haifa 1963, p. 1.

419. Adolf Osterloh, *Report from Civilian Crew Members on North German Lloyds' Donau*, Kristian Ottosen,

"On Such a Night: The History of the Deportation of Jews from Norway," Oslo 1994, pp. 67-72.

420. Knut Rød's Commentary to Report to Oslo Police Station, Department of Collaborators. Pub. by Assistant Detectives Thorbjørn Frøberg and Knut Eberling. The Campaign against the Jews, L-sak Oslo pkm. D 4084, National Archives.

421. Note by State Police Chief Karl A. Martinsen, Evacuation of the Jews, Oslo on November 27, 1942, L-sak Oslo pkm., D 2479, National Archives.

422. Ibid.

423. Ibid.

424. Knut Rød's Commentary to Report to Oslo Police Station, Department of Collaborators. Pub. by Assistant Detectives Thorbjørn Frøberg and Knut Eberling. The Campaign against the Jews, L-sak Oslo pkm. D 4084, National Archives.

425. Note by State Police Chief Karl A. Martinsen, ibid.

426. Ragnvald Kranz, Witness Statement 11.28.46, L-sak Oslo pkm. D 4094, National Archives.

427. Journal for Elias Lasnik, L.nr. 1725/1942., J.nr. 90/XI. Lovisenberg Hospital, Oslo City Archives.

428. Interview Edith Lunder.

429. Document 23, L-sak Oslo pkm. D 4094, National Archives, Oslo.

430. Document 3, ibid.

431. Document 10, p. 7, ibid.

432. *Document Collection on "The Deportation of Jews from Norway to Auschwitz,"* comp. by T. Friedmann, Haifa 1963, p. 3.

433. Interview Edith Lunder.

434. Interview Fride Wilhelmsen.

435. Interview Edith Lunder.

436. Interview Inger-Johanne Østerbø.

437. Transcript of Record Book, December 2, 1942, File 95/C, Box 955, Reparations Office for Confiscated Assets 1942-50, National Archives.

438. Interview Steinar Olav Steinarson.

439. Interview Jannike Eckhoff, Inger Holtung.

440. *Meldungen aus Norwegen*, No. 49, December 15, 1942, Norway's Resistance Museum.

441. "These Students of Fagerborg School Gave Their Lives for Norway in the War 1940-1945." Pamphlet, Oslo n.d.

442. School Council May 7, 1942, School Council Register, August 1941-11/13 1959, Fagerborg School.

443. Joron Pihl, "Monuments and Counter-Monuments," *Nytt Norsk Tidsskrift*, No. 2 2002, p. 141f.

444. Berit Nøkleby and Guri Hjeltnes, *Children During the War*, Oslo 2000, p. 269f.

445. Interview Inger Becker.

446. Ibid.

447. Candidatus theologiæ is a Norwegian degree ranking between a Master and a Ph.D. in Theology.

448. Herlof Kløvstad (ed.), *Sinsen High School, 1936-1964*, Oslo 1964, p. 57.

449. Interview Inger Becker.

450. Swedish Consulate General, Oslo December 14, 1942, No. 1433 HP 21 An, UD 1920 Years' Dossier System, Volumes 181, 181, National Archives of Sweden.

451. Karlstad's Defense Area, Ink d 9/12 1942 Dnr III:205, P 40 L, UD 1920 Years' Dossier System, Volumes 181, 182, National Archives of Sweden.

452. The Ship Departs at 15.00. *Document Collection on "The Deportation of Jews from Norway to Auschwitz,"* comp. by T. Friedmann, Haifa 1963, p. 10.

453. Swedish Consulate General, Oslo December 3, 1942, HP 21 An, UD 1920 Years' Dossier System, HP 1070-1072, National Archives of Sweden.

454. Kristian Ottosen, "On Such a Night: The History of the Deportation of Jews from Norway," Oslo 1994, Annex 1, Jews Deported from Norway 1940-45.

455. Jenny Bermann to the National Board of Health and Welfare and Certificate from M.B. Braathen, Stockholm 11/23-42, Norwegian Legation, Refugee Office. National Board of Aliens, Registry Office, m. vol. F1ABA:351 Central Dossier for Leopold Bermann, National Archives of Sweden.

456. Interview Elise Bassist.

457. Samuel Steinmann, Lecture January 21, 2003. Center for Studies of Holocaust and Religious Minorities in Norway.

458. Ministry of Foreign Affairs, Stockholm 30 Nov. 1942, N:O 126 HP, 21 An, UD 1920 Years' Dossier System, HP 1070-1072, National Archives of Sweden.

459. Ibid.

460. Berlin December 1, 1942, Swedish Delegation, ibid.

461. Berlin December 4, 1942, Swedish Delegation to Secretary of State S. Søderblom, ibid.

462. Berlin December 19 1942, Swedish Delegation to Secretary General G. Engzell, N:O 190, ibid.

463. *Document Collection on "The Deportation of Jews from Norway to Auschwitz,"* comp. by T. Friedmann, Haifa 1963, p. 10.

464. Ibid. p. 10.

465. Robert Savosnick, February 26, 1946, Ministry of Justice, 1. Civil Affairs Department, B, Legal Statements from Homecoming Norwegian Jews, p. 18, National Archives.

466. Samuel Steinmann, Lecture January 21, 2003. Center for Studies of Holocaust and Religious Minorities in Norway.

467. Ibid., and Ministry of Justice, 1. Civil Affairs Department, B, Legal Statements from Homecoming Norwegian Jews, National Archives.

468. *Document Collection*, ibid., p. 11.

469. Erich Hartmann, *In the Camps*, New York - London 1995, p. 36.

470. Danuta Czech, *Calendar of Events in the Concentration Camp Auschwitz-Birkenau 1939-1945*, Hamburg 1989, p. 25.

471. Moritz Nachstern, January 21, 1946, ibid., p. 10f.

472. Moritz Kahan, March 12, 1946, ibid., p. 23.

473. Kai Feinberg, January 17, 1946, ibid., p. 3.

474. Danuta Czech, ibid., p. 26.

475. Copy of Record Book December 2, 1942, Folder 95/C, Box 955, Reparations Office for Confiscated Assets 1942-50, National Archives.

476. Reparations Office for Confiscated Assets O.J.P. No. 536-45. L Note by Haakon Høst, L-sak, Oslo pkm. H 3335, National Archives. Copy of Registration Book December 2, 1942, ibid.

477. Aage Moe to Advocate Haakon Høst, Oslo December 7, 1942, ibid.

478. Undated form signed Egil Reichborn Kjennerud and letter of April 6, 1943, to the Liquidation Board from Haakon Høst, ibid.

479. The Liquidation Board for Confiscated Jewish Property to Lawyer Haakon Høst, Oslo January 23, 1943, ibid.

480. Annual Census Form December 1, 1943, Hertzbergs gate 7, Oslo Municipality, Oslo Population Register and Statistics Office, Oslo City Archives.

481. Interview Inger-Johanne Østerbø.

482. *Fri fagbevegelse* December 6, 1942.

483. NRK. The Radio Archives cannot completely rule out that the event might have been mentioned in parts of the archives found at BBC. However, the Jewish deportations and the *Donau* are not mentioned in 1942 and 1943 in the part of the sound archive that is catalogued.

484. Cited here from Ole Kolsrud, "Exile-Norway and Jews During World War II," *Historisk Tidsskrift*, Vol. 73, No. 3 1994, p. 304.

485. Ibid., p. 305.

486. Beneath Ink. D. N:o is written "req. by Prime Minister," Stockholm Dec. 3, 1942, n:o 84, HP 21 An, UD 1920 Years' Dossier System, HP 1070-1072, National Archives of Sweden.

487. Legation in Stockholm, Refugee Office, Box 3208, National Archives. Cited here from Ole Kolsrud, "Exile-Norway and Jews During World War II," *Historisk Tidsskrift*, Vol. 73, No. 3 1994, p. 305.

488. Swedish Consulate General, Oslo Dec. 3, 1942, N:o 677, HP 21 An, ibid.

489. Ibid.

490. Prince Charles (Carl) of Sweden, the president of the Swedish Red Cross.

491. Swedish Consulate General, Oslo December 12, 1942, N:o 195, ibid.

492. Ministry of Foreign Affairs, Stockholm, February 25, 143. P.M. Concerning Jews in Norway, ibid.

493. *Document Collection on "The Deportation of Jews from Norway to Auschwitz,"* comp. by T. Friedmann, Haifa 1963, p. 49.

494. Document 7, L-sak Oslo pkm H 3335, National Archives.

495. Document 126, ibid.

496. "Lili Marlene" was originally a German song but was adopted by the British Eighth Army with English lyrics.

497. Report to Oslo Police Station Given by Assistant Chief of Police Kaare Schumann Andersen, July 9, 1945, Doc. 7, p. 6. L-sak Oslo pkm. D 4266, National Archives.

498. Lawyer Haakon Høst, Liquidation Board to Ministry of Finance Oslo February 12, 1944, Folder 95/C, Box 955, Reparations Office for Confiscated Assets 1942-50, National Archives.

499. Ibid.

500. Ibid.

501. Ibid.

502. *Norwegian War Encyclopedia 1940-45*, Oslo 1995.

503. Copy of Court Record, Eidsivating Court of Appeals, October 9, 1945, p. 87. L-sak Oslo pkm. D 4266, National Archives.

504. Ibid.

505. Doc. 117, ibid., *Appeal and Defense Document to Norway's Supreme Court*, p. 7.

506. *Norwegians in Captivity 1940-45*, Oslo 1995.

507. Doc. 117, ibid., *Appeal and Defense Document to Norway's Supreme Court*, p. 6f.

508. Sverre Riisnæs to Karl A. Martinsen, Oslo January 27, 1943, L-sak Oslo pkm. D 4094, National Archives.

509. Tore Pryser, *Hitler's Secret Agents: German Intelligence in Norway 1939-1945*, Oslo 2001, p. 495.

510. Basis of Indictment 27 March 1947, p. 4 and 7. L-sak Oslo pkm. D 4931, National Archives.
511. Ibid.
512. Ibid.
513. Ministry of Justice and the Police, Prison Board, Oslo January 17, 1952 to the Atty. General, L-sak Oslo pkm. D 4031, National Archives.
514. Court Records for Oslo City Court, September 9, 1949, L-sak Oslo pkm. D 4094.
515. Knut Sveri, "The Collaboration Settlement's Strangest Case," in *Lov og Frihet*. Commemorative volume for the 70th birthday of Johs Andenæs, September 7, 1982, Oslo 1982. Per Ole Johansen, *The Police Still Have a Reputation to Protect: Arrests and Deportations of Norwegian Jews in the Fall of 1942*, Institute for Criminology. *Årsrapport* 2000.
516. Document 12, p. 2., L-sak Oslo pkm. D 2479, National Archives.
517. Karlstad Defense Area, Ink d 12/9 1942 Dnr III:205, UD, 1920 Years' Dossier System, HP 1070-1072, National Archives of Sweden.
518. Doc. 12, p 3f., L-sak Oslo pkm. D 2479, National Archives.
519. Ibid.
520. Knut Sveri, ibid., p. 350.
521. The Jewish Campaign. Catalog of Patrols. The Chief of the Criminal Police. Jews in Norway - reg., Ministry of the Police 1940-45, National Archives.
522. Statement by Petter Kittelsby, Mathias Løvstuhagen, Oslo June 6, 1945. Doc. 60, L-sak Oslo pkm. D 4094, National Archives.
523. Ibid.
524. Document 19, p. 8, ibid.
525. Ibid., p. 9.
526. Interview Irene Levin.
527. Statement by Kolbjørn Fjeld, L-sak Oslo pkm. D 4094, National Archives.
528. *Rettstidende, 1946*, p. 890.
529. Court Record for Oslo Court of Appeals, Document 10, p. 9, L-sak Oslo pkm. D 4094, National Archives.
530. Ibid.
531. Ibid.
532. Knut Sveri, ibid., p. 355.
533. Ibid.
534. Doc. 10, p. 3, L-sak Oslo pkm. D 4094, National Archives.
535. Knut Rød to the Department of Collaborators, Oslo December 13, 1946, p. 3, ibid.
536. Doc. 10, ibid., p. 1.
537. Hirden was a special paramilitary organization within the NS and served as the NS's police troops.